M000207544

Dinner for a Dollar

Shelly Longenecker

Print Edition 2018

Copyright © 2018 Shelly Longenecker

All rights reserved. This book or parts thereof may not be reproduced in any form, stored in any retrieval system, or transmitted in any form by any means—electronic, mechanical, photocopy, recording, or otherwise—without prior written permission of the author, except as provided by United States of America copyright law.

Graphics and Design: Courtney Alderton

Food Photography: Megan Longenecker

Author Photography: Colleen Adams

Copy Editor: Angela von Weber-Hahnsberg

Developmental Editor: Megan Fennel

Prepared for publication by Write|Publish|Sell writepublishsell.co

Print ISBN: 978-1948604239

Library of Congress Control Number: 2018966279

1st Edition December 2018

10 9 8 7 6 5 4 3 2 1

Contents

Chapter 1 - Our Story, Your Story

A LITTLE ABOUT ME

When our son was about 4 years old—11 years ago—he was facing a lot of health challenges. He had asthma, stomachaches, reflux, was vomiting over 20 times a day, and eventually developed difficulties swallowing. He pretty much felt sick all the time, despite $350 per months' worth of long-term medications that weren't controlling his symptoms. To make a long and dramatic story very short, we discovered he had a disease of the esophagus called Eosinophilic Esophagitis that was exacerbated by multiple food allergies.

Within days of removing the allergens from his diet, his "asthma" was gone and never returned. Within a few weeks, his swallowing started improving. Within several more weeks, his reflux, stomachaches, and vomiting subsided. We were ecstatic! Our little boy was happy, healthy, and thriving. And, for the first time ever, we were thrust into the reality that food has the power to hurt or heal.

Once we saw the benefits to our son's health, we delved full-force into the allergen-free world of eating. Because our son was so young, we decided that 100% of the food in our home would be free of his allergens—for all four of us in the family —so that he wouldn't have to watch us eat food that he couldn't eat. I distinctly remember the day we got his allergy results. When I showed them to my husband, his first response was, "I guess I'm going to have to find a way to make more money to afford our new grocery bill." Even before we had begun, we accepted the myth that eating an allergen-free diet had to be expensive. We also accepted the myth that in order to eat an allergen-free diet, we had to cook complicated food. So, from the beginning of his diagnosis, we spent a ton of money on groceries and I worked countless hours in the kitchen preparing complicated dishes that focused heavily on substitutions. I spent 2-3 hours every day cooking everything from scratch.

Fast forward several years... we were running a couple of businesses, homeschooling, and having more kids. Our life got busier! I no longer had 2-3 hours a day to be in the kitchen, so we ended up eating out "a lot."

Somewhere along the way, we recognized that we weren't living a financially responsible life. We weren't going into debt, but we were mismanaging our money terribly. We weren't setting aside enough money for taxes—every time taxes were due, we had to scramble to come up with thousands of dollars. We weren't setting aside anything for retirement. So, yeah, we weren't going into debt. But we weren't saving for our future either.

We reached a point where we decided that this was no longer acceptable. We wanted to become financially responsible—to be able to pay all our bills with total peace. To have a large emergency fund— just in case. And we wanted to, one day, have the option to retire with dignity. To accomplish these financial goals, we had to bring our food spending under control.

When we finally stopped to calculate how much we were spending on food, it turned out we were spending $1200 a month on groceries and $800 a month on eating out. This didn't include our toiletries or cleaners. We were spending $2000 a month on food! As a family of four! Looking back, I can see that we were literally eating our retirement.

I needed to get serious about our food bill, so I became a student. I read everything I could find that pertained to food spending. I bought a few budget books I thought might help, but none were specifically geared towards people with food allergies, so I had to adjust a lot of the advice to fit our family. I spent time researching and shopping around to find the best prices for food in my local area.

> "Looking back, I can see that we were literally eating our retirement."

Most importantly, I sat down and evaluated what habits I had created that had gotten our family into the position where we were spending $2000 a month on food. I honestly evaluated my planning habits, my shopping habits, and my cooking habits. By doing this, I was able to see the patterns that led to such extreme spending on food. I used those realizations to develop an entirely new way to think about food, shop for food, and prepare food.

And that is how Dinner for a Dollar was born.

It took some time, but I was able to get our family (which is now a family of six) down to a $720-per-month grocery budget and a $300-per-month eating-out budget. That $720-per-month breakdown comes to $1 per person per meal + $1 per person per day for snacks, or $4 per person per day.

By adjusting how I thought about food, shopped for food, and prepared food, I was able to free up $12,000 a year in our family budget. $12,000... of savings... in 1 year!!! Seriously, it's hard for me to believe that this happened. It's important to note that I did all of this without compromising our food values. I slashed our food budget in half while still feeding my family an allergen-free, whole-food diet with lots of fresh fruits and vegetables that my family will eat, and guests enjoy.

I'm confident that I could lower that even more if I needed to or wanted to. But we have decided as a family that this budget is the right one for us at this time. It balances my time, money, and energy well. To lower it further, I would have to invest more time and energy into our food, and we don't want to do that right now.

When I talk to you about food budgeting, I am *not* talking about feeding your family garbage in order to save a buck or two (or 12,000). I'm talking about helping you feed your family real food on a sensible budget.

I am sharing my system of Dinner for a Dollar with the world because I know it's very easy to get out of control with your food budget, especially if you have whole-food values or you have food allergies in your home. I have a passion for helping other families learn how to think differently, shop differently, and cook differently so they can feed their family nutritious whole foods on a budget that's appropriate for their family. I sincerely want to help other families live a financially responsible life—so that they can get out of debt, save for retirement, and hit their family's financial goals. All of that can start by not spending all your money at the grocery store like we did.

A LITTLE ABOUT AMERICANS
. . . .

When you look at the statistics surrounding the current financial state of the American family, you'll realize none of us are alone in our budgeting woes. 41% of American families carry credit card debt at an average amount of $9,333 per family.[1] Over 60% of American homes don't even

---

1   Value Penguin

even have $1000 in their savings account.2 The average American is exceptionally ill-prepared for retirement. Recent stats show that 10,000 baby boomers are hitting retirement every day and 49% of them have less than $10,000 saved.[2] Leading financial experts agree that everyone should be saving at least 15% of their income in order to retire with dignity, yet only 16% of Americans are saving at that rate.[3] That means that 84% of Americans are not adequately preparing for their retirement years.

These are staggering statistics—some of which we were a part of and you may be, too. The food bill is one of the most flexible line items in a family's budget. I want to help you lower your food bill, so you can rise above these statistics—get out of debt, pay your bills with ease, and have a savings account to provide a buffer when emergencies strike. I want you to lower your food bill, so you can carve out 15% to save for retirement and retire with dignity. By helping you control your food budget, I can help you free up money for the things that are truly important in your life, rather than mindlessly spending it all at the grocery store like I was.

A LITTLE ABOUT YOU

So, what brought you here? You bought this book, so I'm assuming you want to bring your food budget under control. But why? I'd like you to take a moment and think about why you want to make changes to your food budget. What are you hoping to accomplish? What are your goals?

Let's say you can reduce your grocery budget by $300 a month. What will you do with that money? Fund your next summer vacation? Put it towards the 15% you're trying to free up for your retirement? Is it to help you get out of debt? Or to help you continue to stay home with your kids?

---

2   Bank Rate

3   Dave Ramsey

Here's one thing I have learned about money over the years...if you don't tell it where to go, life will spend it for you! Every single time. So, if you work hard to lower your food bill, but don't have a goal for what you will do with that money, you likely won't end up further ahead. You might as well just keep eating it! If, however, you take just a little bit of time right now and decide what you will do with the money you free up by lowering your food bill, you can use these funds to accomplish some meaningful things in your life.

A LITTLE ABOUT THIS BOOK

Dinner for a Dollar is not a menu, it's a mindset. You are not going to find a bunch of recipes or meal plans in this book. What you are going to find are the strategies that I use to feed my family $1 meals. I kept it this way because I want people with any food values to be able to use this system to lower their food bill. If you are vegan, paleo, keto, or if you eat a traditional American diet, you can use the tips, tricks, and strategies found in this book to lower your bill. I also want people with all different food needs to be able to use this system. If you have diabetes, need to lose weight, have food allergies, don't have allergies, or if the allergies in your home are different than the allergies in my home, you can use this system to lower your food bill.

If you do have food allergies, you won't find a lot of allergy-specific information in this book because, as I stated, this is a book on how to shop differently, not one that will show people specifically what to cook. (I did, however, write one entire chapter for my fellow peeps with allergies. I highly recommend, if you have food allergies, to start with Chapter 13)

I am not a dietitian, a nutritionist, a food coach, a health coach, a trainer, an allergist or a physician. I'm not qualified in any way to help you make the best food choices for your family. If you need help choosing the best food to meet the specific needs of your family, you need to speak a professional. I have set food values for our family based on our medical needs and my personal research. My personal definition of healthy food is simple—healthy food = whole food. You likely have a different definition for healthy food. And that's okay. Dinner for a Dollar is not a health food plan. This system exists solely to help reduce YOUR food costs for YOUR family, based on YOUR food values.

I hope you see the concepts in this book as a buffet of options. I am going to share with you 11 steps that you can take to reduce your overall food budget. You do not have to do all of these! You can take a few of these tips, make a few simple changes, and save some money. Heck! Even if you have no available time to invest right now in reducing your grocery budget, you can still take two of these tips and lop a noteworthy amount off your food bill.

If you are like I was and you have a completely and ragingly out-of-control food budget, and you are ready to make some serious changes, then you can implement the whole Dinner for a Dollar system and will likely save several hundred dollars a month—perhaps even cut your food bill in half.

Here's how we're going to do it:

1. **We're going to talk about planning.**
2. **We're going to talk about how you cook.**
3. **We're going to talk about how you shop.**

As you go through the book, you are going to see sections set apart called "Action Points"... you can't miss them because they're set apart by a large orange box and the words "Action Points" are in Super-Sized font.

When you get to them, this is when you are supposed to STOP reading and take ACTION! Do not skip over these sections!!!! They are the centerpiece of the Dinner for a Dollar System and are mission critical for you to maximize your savings. You need to answer the questions, do the exercises, and make the plans. If you read the book without completing these sections, you simply will not yield the same benefit. So, trust me… stop when you get to these sections, and take the time to complete them. Your grocery bill will thank you!

ACTION POINT

1. TAKE SOME TIME RIGHT NOW TO ANSWER THESE QUESTIONS:

- Why am I here—reading this book?
- What is my goal?
- What am I going to do with the money that I free up from food savings?

2. HONESTLY EVALUATE THE AMOUNT OF TIME YOU HAVE AVAILABLE RIGHT NOW TO MAKE CHANGES TO YOUR FOOD SYSTEM:

"Girl! I have like *no* time right now at all—I am not even sure why I bought this book!"

- Read chapters 1-3, and then stop.
- Come back to it later when you free up more time or energy in your life.
- "I've got some time I can devote to this, but not a lot."
- Read chapters 1-5, and then stop."I don't have a lot of time, but we are dying over here, and I have got to get this under control. Show me the whole enchilada."
- Start at the beginning and don't cheat! Do all the steps and all the exercises.

3. TAKE A MOMENT RIGHT NOW TO LOOK AT YOUR SCHEDULE OVER THE NEXT COUPLE OF WEEKS AND SLOT IN SOME TIME TO DEDICATE TO LOWERING YOUR FOOD BUDGET.

If you're anything like me, if it's not on your calendar, it won't happen. And this is too important for you to allow that. So, grab your pen and your calendar, and carve out a little time. I recommend about an hour per chapter.

FREE BONUS MATERIAL!

To follow along with us in the Dinner for a Dollar (DFAD) journey, download free resources, and join the club, be sure to follow the link below and use the code. Your DFAD code is the key to access all the most current material and programs available from DFAD.

Dinnerforadollar.co/member

Code: 55133178326

Part 1:
Financial Plan

Chapter 2 – The 'B' Word

Okay, you're probably thinking, "Are you seriously going to start with the 'B' word?"

Sorry, but yes, I am. A budget. You need a budget. Setting a budget for your food costs is so basic that you may be tempted to skip over this step and rush on to the "real savings ideas." Don't do that! Stay here! Having a set budget for your food needs is at the cornerstone of controlling your food costs and making your money work for you.

If you haven't established a set budget for your overall food costs (groceries and eating out), I can tell you this—it is the primary reason your costs are higher than you would like. Without a boundary, you don't know when to stop. Imagine a football game with no lines on the field. Just green grass for miles. People wouldn't know where to play—they wouldn't know how to strategize. More importantly, they wouldn't know if they were winning or losing. This is how it is when we live without a budget. We need these financial parameters to help guide us. To help us strategize. To know when we are #outofbounds and to know when we need a penalty!

SO, WHAT'S A BUDGET?

A budget is simply a plan that tells your money where to go.

That's it—it's you, telling your money where to go. You—you're in charge.

Not the budget. If there is a time when your budget isn't working for you, you can change it! It's there to serve you and help you meet your financial and life goals.

I'm not entirely sure what it is, but whenever people hear the word 'budget,' they seem to shut down. It really seems to carry a negative feeling to it—something like shackles or a ball and chain. Like, somehow, you are a slave to the budget. I think many people miss that a budget puts *YOU* in charge of your money and, ultimately, gives you financial freedom— not bondage. I'm not sure about you, but I would much rather be in charge of my own money than let life dictate where my money will go.

Without a budget, let me tell you who's in charge: NOT YOU!!! Life, Murphy, the IRS, strategic marketing campaigns designed to get you to make mindless purchases, your kids —any one of them is in charge, but not you. If you don't tell your money where to go, it will all leave. Every single time. I promise you.

I feel like I have yelled here for a bit, so let me back it down. As you can tell, I am passionate about budgets. We spent so many years eating our retirement. I don't want the same thing to happen to you.

We've established why a budget is important... now you're probably asking the million-dollar question....

WHAT SHOULD MY BUDGET BE?
....

You'll probably be annoyed to hear that I can't tell you what your budget should be. Frustrating, I know! I wish I could. It would make everything so much easier. But let's take a minute and think about all the variables that go into food budgets:

- **Total dollars available**
- **Household size**
- **Ages of the people in your home**
- **Appetites**
- **Food preferences**
- **Food values**
- **Dietary needs**
- **Location and cost of living**
- **How much time someone has available to save money with food**

If you and I share all these above circumstances, but one of us has four kids aged 12 to 18, and the other one has two kids aged 6 and under, our food budgets are not going to be the same. If one of us lives in Iowa, and the other lives in San Francisco, our food budgets are not going to be the same. I'm sure you can see what I mean. Choosing a food budget is not an exact science. No one can tell you exactly what your budget should be. And you probably won't even be able to determine the ideal budget for your family right away. I had to play with our budget for a while to get us to our sweet spot.

So, if no one can tell you what your budget should be, how do you determine how much you should spend on food?

To get you in the ballpark, you need to start by looking at three factors:

1. Your financial goals
2. The time, money, and energy you have available to spend on food
3. Your food values

1. WHAT ARE YOUR FINANCIAL GOALS?

What are you trying to accomplish here? Maybe you just started Dave Ramsey and need to get out of debt as fast as possible. Maybe you want to stay home with your new baby and need to slash your budget to be able to afford that. Maybe you need to free up an extra $100-200 a month to hit your 15% retirement goals. Maybe you want to fund a family vacation. Maybe you are scraping by and desperate to lower your food bill just to keep a roof over your head. Starting with your financial goals is a critical step in choosing your food budget.

ACTION POINT

If you didn't do this in Chapter 1, take some time right now to figure out why you bought this book.

- **What are you trying to accomplish?**
- **What are you spending now?**
- **How much do you need to lower your food costs to hit your other financial goals?**

---

2. HOW MUCH TIME, MONEY, AND ENERGY DO YOU HAVE AVAILABLE?

For me, the goal *isn't* to spend as little as I possibly can on food for my family: my goal is to spend as little as I can while also honoring our food values, honoring my time and energy AND serving my family food that we (almost) all enjoy (almost) all the time.

There are many things I could do to shave more off our food bill. But, to do that, I would have to either compromise our food values or spend more time/energy than I am interested in spending on food. I don't want to spend all day in the kitchen. I don't want to spend time clipping coupons. I don't want to drive to 37 different stores to save money.

Currently, our budget has enough freedom for me to pass on some of the things that I could be doing to save even more money. Our family's budget is now to the point that it is nearly a perfect balance of my resources—time, money, and energy. **ONLY YOU** can determine what is the perfect number to balance those three things for you.

ACTION POINT

Do you need more time, more money, or more energy? In a perfect world, you could have all three...*heavy sigh*...but not here. Here, you must prioritize these resources.

Take a moment and think about which of these is in shortest supply in your life. Which are you most desperate to have? Prioritize the following in order of their importance to you:

Time

Money

Energy

Keep these priorities in mind as you decide on your budget. The more time and energy you have available to spend on food, the lower your budget can be.

---

3. DETERMINE YOUR FOOD VALUES

Food values are the things that are most important to you in your food life. For example, I would state my food values this way—
I want my meals to:

- be simple and tasty
- use whole foods

- include lots of fresh produce
- be allergen-free
- cost $1 per person

I use these values to form all my meals. Each of us comes to the table with different food values. DFAD is a judge-free zone. We honor your food values, so no judgement here. Your food values are what they are. Our job here is to help you lower your food costs as much as possible with these values in mind.

You need to know your food values before you choose your budget, because they will heavily influence your final budget.

ACTION POINT

Take a moment to jot down your food values. What is most important to you in your food life?

TIME TO PICK A NUMBER

It's time to choose your budget for your family. Let's look at three different ways you can decide on your budget.

1. TAKE WHAT YOU ARE SPENDING RIGHT NOW, AND REDUCE IT IN INCREMENTS, UNTIL YOU CAN NO LONGER FEED YOUR FAMILY ACCORDING TO YOUR FOOD VALUES WITH THE AMOUNT OF TIME AND ENERGY YOU HAVE AVAILABLE.

I've already told you that years ago, we were spending $1200 on groceries and $800 on eating out each month. We now spend $720 on groceries and $300 on eating out. We did not trim nearly $1000 off our food costs overnight! We would have thought we were going to starve to death if I had done that.

Initially, I knew we were completely out of control, so I chopped $300 a month off the top right away. I kept it there for months, to make sure I could sustain that. Over time, we have lowered it little by little until we got to where we are today.

If you choose this method, you can do it like we did and lop off a huge amount right away. Or you can take off $10, $15, $25, $50, or $100 a month and keep doing that until you get to an ideal number you can sustain. For me, an ideal number is one that balances my time, money, and energy with our food values.

2. PICK A NUMBER BASED ON WHAT'S AVAILABLE WHEN CONSIDERING YOUR CURRENT OVERALL BUDGET.

To do this, look at your income against all your bills, and ask yourself this:
Without making more money, reducing other expenses, or going into debt, how much money do you have available to spend on food?

This is probably the best method for you if you have a fixed budget with a lot of expenses and not a lot of wiggle room.

3. YOU CAN PICK A NUMBER BASED ON STANDARDS SUGGESTED BY FINANCIAL OR FOOD EXPERTS, OR BY USING DEMOGRAPHIC RESEARCH, AND THEN ADJUSTING IT AS NEEDED.

Here are some top resources you can use as a guide when choosing your food budget:

• Dave Ramsey recommends families spend 10-15% of their take-home pay on food.   www.daveramsey.com

• Mr. Money Moustache spent $166/month per person in his home in 2016.   www.mrmoneymustache.com

• America's Cheapest Family spends $50 per person per month.   moneysmartfamily.com

• According to the U.S. Department of Labor, the average American household spends 7% of their income on groceries and 6% on eating out.   www.ers.usda.gov

• The USDA has 4 tiers of food budget recommendations: Thrifty, Low, Moderate, and Liberal. They give a suggestion for each person based on their age and gender. To give you a point of reference, for our family of six with kids aged 17, 15, 8, and 5, the USDA recommends a food budget of $924/month for the Thrifty plan, $1210/month for the Low Plan, $1498/month for the Moderate plan, and $1810/month for the Liberal plan.

• To find the USDA recommendations for your family, you can see the chart here: www.cnpp.usda.gov/sites/default/files/CostofFoodMay2018.pdf

• The national average for the Supplemental Nutrition Assistance Program (SNAP—a food assistance program for lower-income families) is $34 per person per week. If our family of six were to receive the national average amount, it would be $816/month.   www.fns.usda.gov/snap/

• My standard is $1 per person per meal + $1/day per person for snacks = $120/month per person. For our family of six, that is a budget of $720/month. You can see that my standard falls far below the USDA Thrifty plan and below the average SNAP allotment, but way above America's Cheapest Family.

The advantage of using someone else's suggestion for a food budget is that you don't have to put a lot of thought or planning into your number. Just choose one and try it out - adjust it up or down as needed. The downside to this method is that the numbers suggested by someone else simply may not work for you. For instance, my number of $1 per person per meal may not be possible in a high-cost-of-living area like Alaska or Hawaii. So, if you do this, be flexible and willing to adjust it accordingly.

Bottom line from this chapter...

YOUR BUDGET NEEDS TO BE BASED ON YOUR FAMILY!

It needs to reflect your food values, weighed against the balance of your available time, money, and energy.

ACTION POINT

1. TO DETERMINE YOUR IDEAL BUDGET, IT IS HELPFUL TO CALCULATE THE AMOUNT YOU'RE CURRENTLY SPENDING ON FOOD AND USE THAT AS A STARTING POINT. THIS ISN'T ABSOLUTELY NECESSARY, SO IF YOU DON'T HAVE DIGITAL RECORDS OF THIS OR IF THIS STRESSES YOU OUT, YOU CAN SKIP THIS STEP.

- If you have 15 minutes and you use debit and/or credit cards to pay for groceries, or you use a budgeting software, you should have a digital record of your grocery spending. Check your records to see what you have been averaging on groceries over the last 3-6 months.

2. NEXT UP, YOU WANT TO WORK ON CHOOSING A STARTING POINT FOR YOUR NEW FOOD BUDGET.

- If you only have 5 minutes, pull out your calendar and schedule a time to choose your new food budget.
- If you have an 30 minutes to an hour, sit down with a cup of coffee and choose a budget for your family's food needs. Remember, it doesn't have to be perfect. This is just a starting point. You can adjust it down the road. If you are married, I suggest involving your spouse in this decision-making process.

Chapter 3 - Use Cash

The simplest thing you can do to reduce your food budget is to set a budget and then exclusively use cash at the grocery store. If you are completely slammed in life and have zero time to make changes to how you think about, shop for, and prepare food, if you at least set a budget and use only cash for your groceries, you can save a good bit of money on your food costs. We covered making a budget in the last chapter. Now, let's talk about using cash at the grocery store.

There exists a large amount of debate about whether people spend more money when using a card vs. using cash. I took a bunch of time and personally read all the research I could find. After reading it, I feel comfortable stating that most people spend more when they swipe a card vs. paying with cash—even when they use debit or when they use credit and pay off their credit card in full every month. Key word here is "most." There definitely are people who can be disciplined enough to strictly follow their budget while using cards, but I believe this is the minority. I believe the cards are truly stacked against us to increase our spending when swiping.

If you are a research geek like me, you can read two comprehensive blogs compiling research studies done on how consumer spending changes with payment type.

- https://www.nerdwallet.com/
  blog/credit-cards/credit-cards-
  make-you-spend-more/
- https://www.valuepenguin.com/credit-cards/credit-card-spending-
  studies

For the normal people out there, here is a synopsis from those studies. Researchers looked at several different shopping scenarios. In all of them, they found that, on average, people spent more when using a card than when using cash. Numbers are all over the board—ranging from 13% to 83% more spent when using a card vs. using cash. At this time, it is impossible to determine *exactly* how much more the average person spends when paying with a card vs. paying with cash, because there was so much variation depending on the circumstances. For the purposes of my book, I am going to pick a figure of 15% to use in my examples. I'm choosing this because it's at the very bottom of the range of the numbers that have been shown to be true in other industries. But, understand that it's speculative in nature. No one has studied grocery habits specifically. So, we really don't know *for sure* that you'll spend less by switching to cash at the grocery store. I can, with certainty, say that the research suggests that the average person will spend less when paying with cash. How much less? We don't really know.

I can also tell you, with certainty, that we slashed our grocery budget by setting a budget and switching to cash. It created a limit—that I could see and feel—at all times. There was no cheating for me. If you currently pay for your groceries with a card, even if you pay it off every month, I want to challenge you to try paying exclusively with cash and see if it helps you stick to your budget. Give it a whirl. I can almost promise you it will be worth it.

If you could save 15% by switching to cash vs. cards, would you consider making the switch? It doesn't seem like much, but let's translate those potential savings into the real world.

If you spend $1000 a month on groceries right now, and you set a budget and switch to cash, you could potentially save $150/month without making any other changes. If you are currently spending $800 a month, you could save $120/month by setting a budget and switching to cash. If you are currently spending $600 a month, you could save $90/month by switching to cash. If you are currently spending $400 a month, you could save $60/month by switching to cash.

I know I'm a grocery/money geek, but doesn't this potential savings just blow you away??!! Such a small change to create such a large potential savings.

Researchers aren't exactly sure why using cash typically leads to spending less, but I'm going to make a couple of guesses based on my own experience.

First, pulling out a set, budgeted amount of cash each pay period, putting it in an envelope, and only using that to pay for groceries serves as a very *visual* reminder of my limits. I can visually see what I have left. With a debit or credit card, I can't see my limits. Emotionally, it feels limitless. I know it isn't, but it feels like it is.

This is especially helpful for me when I go to multiple stores. When I am using my debit card, it is super easy to lose track of how much I've spent for the month after making several stops. Using cash makes it simple. I don't have to track anything.

Secondly, if I only ever use the cash that I've pulled out, it is impossible to overspend. When paying with a card, it is very easy to justify being $5, $10, $20 over budget. I say to myself, "That's no big deal. I can shuffle this or that to make up for it." And, if this happens once or twice, it really is no big deal. But, if it happens many times, compounded over time, these small overages make a real difference for my financial future.

Thirdly, there is something very tangible and physical about the cost of goods when you hand over cash, that's absent when you swipe a card. You FEEL a $200 grocery trip way more when you hand over two hundred-dollar bills, in a way that you don't when you swipe a card.

Cards are so much more convenient than cash, so you may be making some arguments in your head against using cash. Let's take a moment and address those possible objections now.

ACTION POINT

Stop here and ask yourself – If you knew you could save $60, $90, $120, or $150 per month on your food bill by simply setting a budget and paying with cash, would you do it?

---

1) I'M WORRIED MY CASH WILL GET STOLEN.

Okay. This is solid. I don't want my hard-earned cash getting stolen either! We're supposed to be saving money here, not losing money. Stop and ask yourself, in your entire lifetime, how many people do you know who have had their cash stolen—either from their wallet or from their home?

I only know of two instances. In my 44 years of life. Now, of course this happens. It really does. But the chances of someone skimming your debit card number from the machine at the grocery store are actually much higher. So, honestly, I consider the risk of cash getting stolen to be quite small.

2) I'M WORRIED I WILL LOSE MY CASH.

I feel you here. When we switched to cash, I had to develop a system for storing and using my cash. It was a new thing—so I had to figure out how to handle it. When will I get it from my bank? Where will I store it between payday and the day I go to the store? When it's in my wallet, how will I know which cash is for groceries and which cash is for other things?

These are things you'll have to work out—I'll have you address them in a moment. But it's simple not to lose your cash if you have a system for it—you will need to find a secure spot to store it and keep it there until you need it.

3) I GET POINTS WHEN I USE MY CREDIT CARD.

This one was SO hard for me to let go of. To get over this, I had to realize that, on average, the rewards I would get wouldn't offset the increased amount of money spent when using a card. On average, card rewards pay out $0.01 for every $1 spent. So, when you spend $10,000, you yield approximately $100 in rewards. On first glance, that's very appealing! Who doesn't want $100 in "free" money? Am I right? But if I spend 15% more when using a card than when using cash, it's actually costing me money to use a card. That $10,000 spent potentially represents $1,500 more in expenses, to receive that $100 in rewards. This doesn't seem as good, when I look at it that way. Now, I know for a fact that there are people who use cards in an incredibly disciplined manner—who spend exactly the same with a card as they would with cash—and then they cash in on those rewards. Good for them!!! They should definitely keep doing this. However, you have to know that those people are the minority. For the majority of us, swiping a card represents a significant increase in the amount of money spent. Far above the rewards that you will earn. In short, for most people, even when you factor in the rewards, using a card costs you more money than spending cash—even if you pay it off in full every month and never pay a late fee or interest.

4) I'M WORRIED I WILL FORGET IT WHEN I GO TO THE STORE.

Drive home and get it. Really. You will only do this once, and then you'll remember it every time.

5) I'M WORRIED WE WILL SPEND IT ON OTHER THINGS. WHENEVER I HAVE CASH IN MY WALLET, IT GETS SPENT BY ME OR MY FAMILY.

Store your grocery envelope in a special place. Don't keep it in your wallet. This helps me solve this problem completely.

6) I'M WORRIED I WILL OVERSPEND AT THE CASH REGISTER AND WILL NEED TO TAKE STUFF OFF. THIS WILL BE SO EMBARRASSING!

This is going to happen. Especially at first. Once you get better, it will happen less and less. Now I know—within about $20 – what my grocery bill is going to be without doing any tallying while I go. This just comes with experience and time. In the meantime, you are going to overspend and will need to take stuff out, if you don't do some type of tallying while you shop. Keep in mind that the store is there to serve you. The cashier is being paid hourly. So, don't worry about them. Decide now not to let it bother you. Decide now that hitting your financial goals (trip to Disney, staying home with your kids, being able to retire before 70) are more important than not being embarrassed at the checkout.

There are three simple ways you can avoid having to remove items that have already been scanned—the first is the method I personally use:

- **As you are loading items onto the belt, prioritize your items.**

In the first group, put your necessities. In the second group, put the optional items—loosely in order from most important to least. Ask for a total after the cashier scans everything from the first group. Then, you will know how much you have left to spend for the more optional items.

Watch the total carefully and have her stop when she reaches your limit. This only takes the cashier a couple of extra minutes, and I have NEVER once had anyone get annoyed with this. I'll usually tell the cashier how much I have to spend, so we can be watching that total together. It's like a game we play. This is a pretty simple method. And much less embarrassing than having to pull out items that have already been scanned. I use this method mostly because I'm too lazy to tally while I go.

- **Buy a hand-held clicker - Use this to click the button for every dollar you put in the cart.**

Round up or down as appropriate. But, even with rounding, this will give you a solid estimate of where you're at – without drawing any attention to yourself or your budget while you are shopping. This is probably the best method for you if you want to be as discreet as possible.

- **Physically total as you go.**

You can use a calculator or a clipboard. This is the most accurate way to know your total as you are shopping, but it's probably also the most time-consuming.

Now that I've helped you see the importance of using cash at the grocery store, and helped you bust some myths about using cash, let's go through the practical steps I take to use cash for groceries. I know it seems basic, and most of you probably don't need to read this part, but I'm including it for those who like to see the nitty-gritty.

You can choose to do this differently, but what I do is pull out our budgeted amount for food at each paycheck. I put my grocery money in an envelope labeled "Groceries," our family eating-out money in an envelope labeled "Eating Out," and my husband's work eating-out money in an envelope labeled "Work Eating Out." We get paid on the 1st and the 15th. Our monthly grocery budget is $720 ($1 per person per meal + $1 per person per day for snacks). So, each pay period, I take out $360 cash and put that in our grocery envelope. I have an extra-special spot where I store this grocery envelope. When it's shopping day, I grab the envelope on my way out the door. When I get home, I put the envelope back in my special spot and keep it there until my next grocery trip. Super simple. And super effective.

Hopefully this chapter helped you consider the potential benefits of using cash for your groceries and inspired you to give it a try. Of course, as with all things in my book, you can disagree with me and do whatever you want. I love that personal finances are personal, and that **we can each make our own decisions about what works best for us.** We have seen so much benefit from switching over to cash that I simply couldn't leave that suggestion out of the book! If you're on the fence, jump in and give it a try! Find out for yourself if it is a strategy that can work for you.

ACTION POINT

If you've decided to give cash a whirl, jump right in and take the following steps:

1. MAKE YOUR SPECIFIC CASH PLAN.

If you cheated and skipped the exercise in Chapter 2 about setting your grocery budget, take some time right now and set your budget.

- What is your monthly budget for your food costs?
- How much will you pull out per pay period?
- How and when are you going to get your cash out?
- Where will you keep it?
- How will you remember to bring it with you?

2. HOW ARE YOU GOING TO KEEP TRACK OF YOUR GROCERY TOTAL AS YOU ARE SHOPPING?

Which of the 3 methods will you use? Or have you come up with your own strategy? If you are going to use the clicker, take a moment and buy it now.

If you are going to total as you go, decide specifically how you are going to do that, and gather whatever supplies you will use. Do you need a clipboard? Do you need a calculator?

Part 2 –
Food Plan 101

Ch 4 – Make a (Food) Plan

Now that you know how many dollars you're going to spend, I want to help you figure out what you're going to spend them on. You need a plan. To eat the best food for the best prices, you will have to be proactive and intentional with your food choices. Planning on the front end saves you time, money, and energy on the back end. Putting your planning day and shopping day on your calendar is the first step.

So how do you build a food plan?

If you're not used to meal planning, start with a simple system that resonates with you and try it out for a while—then tweak it as you go. Like your budget, your meal planning system works for **YOU,** not the other way around. If it isn't working for you, make changes to it, or kick it to the curb and try a different way. All this to say—be flexible and adaptable.

I'll start by showing you how I make my food plan for our family. This planning system may or may not work for you. Maybe you'll find you need to plan your food differently. Or maybe you need to outsource the planning and pay someone else to do it. That's okay! Any planning system will be better than none! There are a lot of excellent meal planning services out there.

For my food planning, I start by putting my planning day and my shopping day on my calendar. Planning our meals and shopping for our food are scheduled events in my life. If I don't put them on my calendar, I find I don't prioritize them, and I end up shopping on an as-needed basis, making more trips, spending more money, spending more time and having fewer options for meals.

My food plan consists of 4 steps:

Step 1: Do a complete food inventory
Step 2: Make a meal plan
Step 3: Make a grocery list
Step 4: Gather the things needed for Shopping Day

STEP 1 – DO A COMPLETE FOOD INVENTORY

At the start of every food plan, I always take a complete inventory of all the food I have on hand. I take stock of everything in the fridge, freezer, and pantry. I mark every item I have and the quantity of each item.

I'm pretty sure I can already hear you saying, "WHAT??… Has this girl gone crazy? She writes down all the food in her house before she goes shopping—every time?" Well, I mean, maybe I have lost my mind. I have been parenting for 17 years. But, seriously, no, I'm not crazy—at least not about this. Doing a complete food inventory every time before I shop has transformed my food budget. It is the key way that I have reduced my food waste. I only added this step a couple of years ago, and it makes me wonder how I lived without it. Let me tell you what your food inventory will tell you.

1) YOUR FOOD INVENTORY WILL TELL YOU WHAT FOOD YOUR FAMILY NEVER EATS!

When you know what your family never eats, you will know never to buy it—this reduces food waste!

2) YOUR FOOD INVENTORY WILL ALSO TELL YOU WHAT YOUR FAMILY *DOES* EAT AND *HOW MUCH* OF IT THEY EAT.

When you know what your family does eat and how much of it they eat, you can buy the right food in the right quantities—this saves extra trips to the store.

3) YOUR FOOD INVENTORY WILL ALSO TELL YOU A DIRTY LITTLE SECRET—IT WILL TELL YOU WHAT YOU, THE FAMILY CHEF, *WON'T* PREPARE.

I call it the "food of good intentions." Maybe you saw it on Pinterest, or a friend told you all about its amazing qualities, and you bought it with good intentions—but will never get around to actually cooking it. For me, this is quinoa, flax seed, and chia seeds. I have bought these items time and time again, and rarely used them. So. much. waste. Everyone has "food of good intentions," but it's different for each of us. There's nothing wrong with this list. The only thing wrong with it is if you're not honest about it, and keep buying food that you won't prepare. When you stop buying "food of good intentions" —this saves you money and reduces mom guilt.

I've included a sample inventory list that you will find at the end of this chapter.

STEP 2 – MAKE A MEAL PLAN

After I finish my inventory, I make a Meal Plan. I plan my meals based on two things: 1) the meat I already have in my freezer, and 2) any ingredients I need to use up.

I'll cover purchasing food at the best possible prices in Chapter 8. For the purposes of this chapter on making a meal plan, you need to know that meat is the most expensive part of our meal plan. Because of this, sourcing meat at rock-bottom prices is the primary way I reduce my per-meal price. When I'm shopping, I always keep an eye out for clearance meats, and buy as much as I can use or safely store.

I never, ever pay full price for meat. And I very rarely even pay sale prices for meat. I strictly hold out for clearance pricing. This method is very effective at lowering my per-meal pricing. However, it is an incredibly inconsistent method for obtaining meat. I never know when I will be able to buy it. So, when it comes to meal planning, I don't just decide that we want beef tenderloin on our menu for the week, and then go to the store and buy the beef for that meal. Instead, I go to my freezer, see what meat I have on hand, and create meals around that.

After I do my complete inventory, I know exactly what meat I have available to work with AND I know what other ingredients in my fridge or pantry that I need to focus on using up. I use these items as the launching point for the meals I will prepare for my family that week. Here are some of the ways that I pick the meals for my menu:

- If feeling creative and inspired, I just bang out two weeks' worth of meals from a mental list of food I know my family likes...this is rare.
- Use past meal plans as inspiration. I have a folder with my favorite recipes and my past meal plans in it. I pull those out and use them to build my next meal plan. This is my favorite way to build my meal plan, as the hard work is already done for me.
- Ask family members for 2-3 meals that they would like to eat over the next two weeks. When I do this, I require them to give me a set number. It's awesome because it's a quick source of 10-15 meal ideas for me.
- Do a web search for 'what can I make with (ground beef, or pork butt, or ham, or whole chickens, or [whatever]).' It's shocking how helpful this is when I am stuck on how to use up what I have on hand.
- In the past, I used meal planning services. These are helpful if you are really stuck or don't have the time and energy for meal planning.

When I'm making my meal plan, I keep my schedule in front of me and plan around that schedule. I see when we have school events or family celebrations where we may need special food. I see when our schedule is busy, and we need extra-simple food. So, on my meal plan, I write in any special events happening on that day, so I can be mindful of making our schedule work together with our food.

For my meal plan, I write out a plan for lunch and dinner. As you look at my meal plans over time, you will see that lunches, for us, are almost exclusively leftovers or dinners that have been re-purposed. I used to make an entirely separate meal for lunches. Looking back, I just cannot believe I ever did that. When I nixed that habit, I saved so much time in the kitchen! I saved so much energy—fewer things to plan and shop for—fewer dishes to wash. If you haven't been hitting your food budget goals, **I highly recommend purposefully planning leftovers for lunches and seeing if it saves you time and money.** I don't write out a plan for breakfast because we literally eat from a handful of breakfast options. When I do my inventory, I just make sure we are well-stocked with all our breakfast staples.

I've included a meal plan chart that you will find at the end of this chapter.

STEP 3 – MAKE A GROCERY LIST

I only add three things to my list:

1. INGREDIENTS NEEDED TO COMPLETE THE MEALS ON MY MENU

I am mindful of the pricing for ingredients needed to complete meals. If the price for the ingredients needed to complete the meals is too high, I improvise by either nixing the meal and choosing something else OR swapping out the expensive ingredient for something else. I will cover this strategy in the next chapter.

2. ANY STAPLES I NEED

These items are the handful of things I buy almost no matter what the price is.

3. ANY STOCK I NEED TO REPLENISH

I am really strict about pricing when I replenish my stock. Really strict! I try my very best to only replenish stock at rock-bottom pricing. If the item is at a normal sale price and I really need it, I will buy about a 1-month supply. If the item is at rock bottom, I buy as much as I can use or safely store. I cover this in detail in Chapter 8.

I've included a sample shopping list that you will find at the end of this chapter.

STEP 4 – GATHER THE THINGS YOU NEED FOR SHOPPING DAY

My final step in planning is to gather everything I will need on shopping day. I use a clipboard to keep all the things I need in one place. On the clipboard, I clip the following:

- **A shopping list for my main store.** I put this on top.
- **A shopping list for any other stores—including Loss Leaders.** I put this next, so I can quickly reference the price difference between my main store and the Loss Leaders at other stores.
- **My meal plan.** I include this, so I can quickly sub other meals or ingredients if I see that something that I need for my meal plan is coming in too high.
- **My inventory list.** I find it helpful to be able to reference my complete inventory while shopping because my memory is incredibly short these days (can I get a witness???). If I run across an unexpected sale, I can reference how much I have at home to help me decide how many to get.

To capitalize on maximum savings, you must have a plan when going to the store. You can still save a lot of money by using some or all the other steps and skipping this one. But to get the most savings, you need to embrace this one.

If you're not used to making a plan for your shopping trips, making this change will take a little bit more time on the front end. It may be cumbersome at first, but don't get too frustrated.

Stick with it. It will become second nature. And it will save you so much time, energy, and money that you will quickly realize it was worth any effort that you put into it. Personally, I look back now and can't imagine operating without a thorough meal plan. Even if it didn't save me any money, I would do it purely for the time and energy savings—I spend so much less time and energy on food when I have a plan!

ACTION POINT

IF YOU HAVE 5 MINUTES:

· Print out the inventory list, the meal plan & the shopping list. Samples of these are on the next page or for more examples, look in the workbook.

· Locate a clipboard or put one on your shopping list (You can grab one at Goodwill or the dollar store).

IF YOU HAVE 15 MINUTES:

· Do a complete food inventory – write down everything you have.

IF YOU HAVE 30 MINUTES:

· Make your next meal plan.
· Make your next shopping list.

Food Inventory

Fridge

Dairy
___ Milk
___ Butter
___ Cheese
___ _____
___ _____
___ _____

Deli
___ Ham
___ Turkey
___ Hummus
___ Salami
___ _____

Condiments
___ Ketchup
___ Mustard
___ BBQ
___ Mayo
___ Sriachi
___ Ranch
___ Salad Dressing
___ Terriaki
___ Pickles
___ Minced Garlic
___ _____
___ _____
___ _____

Fresh Vegetables
___ _____
___ _____
___ _____
___ _____

Fresh Meat
___ Chicken
___ Beef
___ Pork
___ Fish
___ Turkey
___ Eggs
___ _____
___ _____
___ _____
___ _____

Freezer

Meat
___ Whole Chicken
___ Chicken Legs
___ Chicken Thighs
___ Chicken Breasts
___ Marinated Chicken Breasts
___ Chicken Wings
___ Cooked Chicken
___ Whole Ham
___ Diced Ham
___ Sliced Ham
___ Pork Roasts
___ Pork Tenderloin
___ Cooked Pulled Pork
___ Ground Beef
___ Cooked Ground Beef
___ Ground Turkey
___ Fish
___ Beef Roast
___ Cooked Pulled Beef
___ Steaks
___ Ribs
___ _____
___ _____
___ _____
___ _____

Frozen Fruit/ Veggies
___ Bananas
___ Strawberries
___ Mixed Berries
___ Broccoli
___ Peas
___ Mixed Veggies
___ Potatoes
___ _____
___ _____
___ _____

Other
___ Cooked Rice
___ Ham Bones
___ Chicken Bones
___ Cooked White Beans
___ Cooked Black Beans
___ Cooked Pinto Beans
___ _____
___ _____
___ _____

Pantry

Condiments
___ Ketchup
___ Mustard
___ BBQ
___ Mayo
___ Sriachi
___ Ranch
___ Salad Dressing
___ Terriaki
___ Pickles
___ _____
___ _____
___ _____

Bulk
___ Dry Black Beans
___ Dry Pinto Beans
___ Rice
___ Steel-cut Oats
___ Quick Oats
___ Pasta
___ _____
___ _____
___ _____
___ _____

Pantry Vegetables
___ Sweet Potatoes
___ Potatoes
___ Onions
___ Spaghetti Squash
___ _____
___ _____
___ _____
___ _____

Snack Staples
___ Z Bars
___ Clif Bars
___ Applesauce
___ Rice Rollers
___ Fruit & Nut Bars
___ _____
___ _____
___ _____

Canned
___ Canned Corn
___ Diced Tomatoes
___ Tomato Paste
___ Tomato Sauce
___ Applesauce
___ Veggies
___ Canned Black Beans
___ Canned Pinto Beans
___ Canned White Beans
___ Canned Chilis
___ _____
___ _____
___ _____
___ _____

Baking
___ Olive Oil
___ Coconut Oil
___ Vegetable Oil
___ Egg Replacer
___ Sugar
___ Brown Sugar
___ Flour
___ GF Flour
___ GF Baking Mix
___ GF Pancake
___ Corn Starch
___ Baking Soda
___ Baking Powder
___ Maple Syrup
___ Honey
___ Raw Honey
___ White Vinegar
___ Apple Cider Vinegar
___ Balsamic Vinegar
___ Red Wine Vinegar
___ Spices
___ _____
___ _____
___ _____
___ _____
___ _____

Menu

	MONDAY	TUESDAY	WEDNESDAY	THURSDAY	FRIDAY	SATURDAY	SUNDAY
LUNCH	☐	☐	☐	☐	☐	☐	☐
DINNER							

	MONDAY	TUESDAY	WEDNESDAY	THURSDAY	FRIDAY	SATURDAY	SUNDAY
LUNCH	☐	☐	☐	☐	☐	☐	☐
DINNER							

Shopping List

Vegetables
___ Potatoes
___ Sweet Potatoes
___ Beets
___ Onions
___ Carrots
___ Lettuce
___ Celery
___ Sale Veggies
___ _____
___ _____
___ _____
___ _____
___ _____
___ _____
___ _____
___ _____
___ _____

Dairy
___ Milk
___ Eggs
___ Butter
___ Cheese
___ _____
___ _____
___ _____
___ _____
___ _____

Fruit
___ Apples
___ Bananas
___ Sale Fruit
___ _____
___ _____
___ _____
___ _____
___ _____
___ _____

Condiments
___ Ketchup
___ Mustard
___ BBQ
___ Ranch
___ Pickles
___ Honey
___ _____
___ _____
___ _____
___ _____
___ _____

Bulk
___ Steal Cut Oast
___ Almond Butter
___ _____
___ _____
___ _____
___ _____

Meat
___ Chicken
___ Beef
___ Pork
___ Fish
___ Turkey
___ _____
___ _____
___ _____
___ _____
___ _____
___ _____
___ _____
___ _____
___ _____
___ _____
___ _____

Dry
___ Rice
___ Beans
___ Oats
___ Sugar
___ Brown Sugar
___ GF Flour
___ Spices
___ _____
___ _____
___ _____
___ _____

Deli
___ Ham
___ Turkey
___ Hummus
___ Salami
___ _____
___ _____
___ _____

Frozen
___ Diced Potatoes
___ Mixed Veggies
___ Peas
___ Strawberries
___ _____
___ _____
___ _____
___ _____

Canned
___ Tomatoes
___ Tomato Sauce
___ Applesauce
___ Veggies
___ Beans
___ _____
___ _____
___ _____
___ _____

Chapter 5 – Reduce your trips

THE MORE OFTEN YOU GO TO THE STORE, THE MORE MONEY YOU WILL SPEND.

I clearly remember the day when this reality struck me. I was standing in the kitchen, thinking about food and budgets, and it hit me: "The more often I go to the store, the more money I spend." I distinctly remember feeling like a complete idiot when it hit me. The more I go, the more I spend. **IT WAS SO OBVIOUS!** Why hadn't I thought of this before? How did it take me 20 years of grocery shopping to realize that going to the store less would reduce my grocery bill?

I found my husband, explained my epiphany, and told him I wanted to try to reduce our trips to the store and see if I could save even more money on our groceries. He said, "Hmmm. Seems about right. I think you should try that." So, I did.

At the time of this realization, we were spending about $900/month on groceries (down from the original $1200/month), and I was just beginning to brainstorm ways that I could bring that down even further—while still respecting our food values **AND** my time, energy, and sanity. We were going to the store **ALL. THE. TIME**. I don't know how many times. But, if I had to guess, I could safely estimate that we were going 2-3 times a week. I decided to aim to reduce our trips to one per week. I figured that if I could reduce the number of trips from 2-3 times a week down to one time a week, I would be doing great.

I made the switch right away, and it was **SO HARD** at first. Seriously, I thought I was going to die. We ran out of stuff all the time. I was constantly forgetting ingredients. Reducing my trips to once a week required detailed planning on my part. I had to actually think, ahead of time, of everything I would need for the week! Birthday parties, potlucks, holidays, special events, lunches—for everyone in my family (not just half of them—how do I forget half? No idea...). Oh my gosh!

But I'm here now. So, clearly, I survived the experiment. Not only did I survive, but reducing our trips did, in fact, reduce our budget! We were able to drop and maintain our budget at $800/month—without changing what we ate or where I shopped. The best part was that it came with an added bonus, which I hadn't even thought about: I saved time and energy. Fewer trips to the store = less time shopping. Fewer trips to store = less time thinking about food. Fewer trips to the store = less money spent. Seriously, this isn't rocket science, is it? How had this never occurred to me?

After I mastered one trip per week, I moved my grocery trips to every ten days. I maintained that schedule until I had mastered it. Now, today, I shop every two weeks and have been for over a year. Shopping every two weeks has brought our grocery bill down to $720.

Every two weeks seems to work well for me. It allows me to maximize my savings, minimize my time at the store, and minimize the amount of time I spend thinking about and planning for food, while still allowing us to eat a diet rich in fresh fruits and vegetables. I know that many frugal-food families shop one time a month. I am confident that I could lower my budget more if I moved my shopping to once a month, but we just aren't willing to give up the volume of fresh fruits and vegetables that we eat. I have toyed around with going every three weeks, or with doing a big trip every month, and a produce run every two weeks, but I haven't been willing to experiment with any of those schedules yet, since I am at a good place at the moment.

ACTION POINT

Stop for a moment and ponder these questions:

- **How many times/per week are you shopping now?**

- **If you thought it could save you time, money, and energy, would you be willing to reduce your shopping trips?**

At this point, you may be wondering how you could possibly reduce your trips. Let me start by telling you that if I did it, you can, too! If you are going to the store 2-3 times a week, you probably don't want to start out by switching to twice a month. Only you know yourself and your circumstances, but that's probably too much of an adjustment. You may want to do what I did and start with one time a week, and then possibly move up from there. Or you may decide that once a week is the perfect amount for you and leave it there.

I'm going to share with you how I make the 2-week schedule work for me. You can apply these same strategies to make whatever schedule you choose work for you. The most important thing you need to know about how I make the 2-week schedule work for me is that I make a commitment and a plan.

Here are the strategies I use to keep my (usually) strict 2-week shopping schedule:

1. TRIPS ARE SCHEDULED — ON MY CALENDAR

I already covered this, but it's worth repeating. I schedule, on my calendar—in writing—my grocery shopping day. I also put my planning day on the calendar. I've found that putting my planning day and shopping day on my calendar and notifying my family of the scheduled event makes it something important. I am way more likely to go shopping on my scheduled day if it's on my calendar.

2. THERE IS A DETAILED PLAN

Like I mentioned in the previous chapter, I make a meal plan for our family for the two weeks' time I'll be shopping for. I include our regular meals, snacks as well as anything I need for any special events that are happening in that 2-week time period. I have my calendar beside me when planning, and I take our family schedule into account when making our meal plan. If we have busy times, I adjust what we are eating to accommodate that. From this meal plan, I make a detailed and quantified shopping list. By detailed, I mean that I take into account our schedule and all special events. This way I don't have to make extra grocery runs to account for items needed for forgotten events. By quantified, I mean that once I make my meal plan for the week, I quantify how much of each item we need. Rather than putting "apples" on my list, I put "20 red apples and 10 green apples" on my list, as this is the approximate amount we consume in a 2-week time period. Rather than putting "onions" on my list, I put 8 onions (or however many I need to make the recipes that I'm cooking. I didn't used to do this, but it has been a very helpful small switch. Quantifying my list ensures both that we have enough to make it through the 2-week time period, as well as bringing waste way down by keeping me from buying more than we can consume or safely store in a 2-week time period.

3. WE START BY ASSUMING WE NEED TO USE UP WHAT WE HAVE

Find ways to use up what you have. If you can use what you have and reduce your waste, the food you do have will last longer. We will spend an entire chapter on this later—teaching you some specific ways to do this. But it deserves at least a mention here, because it is an important part of being able to stretch your ingredients until grocery day.

4. BE FOOD FLEXIBLE

Do you know that when a recipe calls for a specific ingredient, you are not required by law to use that exact ingredient? There are no recipe police out there. No one will write you a citation if you don't follow it exactly. Many times, you can swap out ingredients. Or you can delete ingredients and make do without them. You don't have to use the special spice, the specific piece of produce, the exact cut of meat, or even the exact type of meat.

I think of meals more as equations than recipes. I frequently sub one ingredient out for another. This helps me save spontaneous trips to the store when I forget ingredients. I use my equation to quickly sub my missing ingredient for something I do have. Spontaneous trips to the store are budget busters! I will hit more on this topic in the next chapter, so if you don't feel like you can do this yet, don't worry.

5. STRATEGICALLY PLAN MEALS BASED ON PRODUCE SHELF LIFE.

In week 1, we eat meals focused on using our quickest-to-spoil ingredients. This is when we do all our salads and consume any fresh berries or highly perishable produce.

In week 2, we eat meals that focus on vegetables with the longest shelf life. We focus on using fresh produce like: beets, cauliflower, onions, carrots, spaghetti squash, potatoes, sweet potatoes, winter squashes, apples, oranges, and frozen fruits for smoothies.

6. IF YOU ARE SHOPPING AT MULTIPLE STORES, DO YOUR BEST TO HIT THEM ALL IN THE SAME DAY

If you can pull this off, I suggest you give it the old college try. For some of you, this simply isn't possible. I remember those days. If your food plan requires that you hit multiple stores, and you can't hit them in the same day, do still schedule all of your trips. Map it out. When will you go to x store? Y store? How about z? Put them all on your calendar.

I do my VERY, VERY BEST to only shop every two weeks. I really focus on this goal because it helps me keep my budget in check. But, it also dramatically reduces the amount of time and energy I spend thinking about, planning for, and shopping for food. Can I stand before you and say that I never, ever, ever go to the store on unscheduled days??? Ummm, nope! **I am not food perfect.** Really, I'm not. And I don't try to be—and you shouldn't either. But I can say that it is infrequent. And, for sure, spontaneous trips are a fraction of what they were before.

I can also say, with certainty, that the extra effort in planning that I put in on the front end, is absolutely worth it in time, money, and energy savings on the back end. I am convinced that, if you decide to reduce your trips, put them on your calendar, and stick to it, you will spend less time, money, and energy on food as well. Give it a try.

ACTION POINT

If you have 5 minutes, set your shopping schedule for this month.

- **How many times this month will you shop?**

- **Pull out your calendar—write on your calendar which day you are shopping. Write on your calendar which day you are planning.**

If you have 15 minutes, jot down meals your family eats that could rely on fruits and vegetables that can last up to two weeks.

Part 3 –
Food Plan 202

We covered the basics of food planning when we discussed making a plan and reducing your trips on Ch 4 and 5. Now we are going to move on to some other planning strategies I use to reduce the time, money, and energy I spend on food.

Chapter 6 – Be food flexible

Wait a minute... be food flexible. What on earth does that mean? Hang with me for just a minute while I explain. Being food flexible starts out with a friendly and courteous announcement you may have never considered before.

RECIPES CAN BE BUDGET BUSTERS.

They really can be. Let's say I see a recipe for a Flank Steak Spinach Salad and I decide to put it on my meal plan. It seems healthy and fresh and it aligns with my food values, so it goes on the meal plan. The ingredients needed for it go on my shopping list. I get to the store and flank steak is $7.99 a pound. Spinach is in short supply, so it's at the inflated price of $6.99 for a bag large enough to feed my family. The recipe calls for some special spices and fresh oranges for the vinaigrette. Oranges aren't in season and the spices aren't on sale, so I spend $15 on oranges and spices. **Without really thinking about it, I have just spent $30 on a Spinach Flank Steak Salad.**

This is "not" a far-fetched story. It happened to me countless times before I started taking grocery prices seriously. And, I bet it has happened to you as well. This is especially true for things like potlucks, baby showers, birthday parties, or holidays. We get something specific in our mind and, if we aren't willing to be flexible about it, it can cost us more than we want to pay.

To lower your food costs as much as possible, you need to free yourself from the need to perfectly follow a recipe.

While I used to consider recipes a set of rules to follow, I now consider them a suggestion.

You know that if a recipe calls for snow peas, you don't actually *have* to use snow peas, right? You can go crazy and use something like, oh, I don't know... carrots... or broccoli... or peas... or water chestnuts... or zucchini... or cauliflower. For real... there is literally no law about this. No recipe police. No citations. No fines. And no one ever needs to know (I won't tell... I promise).

"If I am not going to be using recipes, what in the heck am I going to be feeding my family?" I thought you would never ask...

Rather than using recipes, I try to think of my meals in terms of an equation.

Not a math equation, but rather a food equation. A food equation is a concept I made up and use all the time in my cooking. It is a combination of foods that I aim to base all meals on. It allows me to freely swap out expensive ingredients with ingredients I can source inexpensively. I form our meals based on this equation. I call it my Food Formula. Here is the Food Formula we follow in our home:

Meat + starch + veggie + veggie + fat + seasonings = my next meal

Since we are new food friends, I will tell you something important about me here at Dinner for a Dollar. I am not a dietitian, a nutritionist, a food coach, a trainer, or a health and wellness coach. I am not here to help you make food choices for your family. I am here to help you save money on the food that you choose to buy for your family. Because I am not a trained food expert, I am not suggesting that the Food Formula listed above is one that anyone should use. I am not suggesting it is healthy. It is what we have chosen to eat based on the research I have done and our family's needs. I only share my Food Formula with you to give an example you can use to determine your own. So, if this food formula doesn't match your food values or the needs of your family, that's A-OK!! Just make your own. I promise not to judge your Food Formula and I hope you don't judge mine either. Dinner for a Dollar is a judge-free zone!

When I form my meals based on that equation, rather than a recipe, it frees me up immensely in the kitchen and I yield savings to my time, money, and energy. Let me share with you the benefits of being food flexible and using a Food Formula in place of recipes:

#1. IT ALLOWS ME TO FREELY SWAP OUT INGREDIENTS... THIS REDUCES MY GROCERY BILL

Let's say that the recipe calls for chicken breasts, but they're not on sale and I have an abundance of chicken thighs on hand. Simple swap. It may change the texture or form of the food, but the end result is the same—feeding my family a tasty, whole food diet on a strict budget. This flexibility allows me to capitalize on food I was able to purchase at deep discounts. When I use ingredients that I have sourced at rock bottom prices, my food bill lowers dramatically over time.

#2. WHEN I AM IN A TIME CRUNCH, USING THE FOOD FORMULA ALLOWS ME TO QUICKLY ASSESS WHAT I HAVE ON HAND TO CREATE A SIMPLE, FAST MEAL... THIS REDUCES MY EATING OUT BUDGET.

Let's say that I am running around like a chicken with my head cut off, haven't planned for anything, it's 4:30 and I have no idea what I am going to make. This is, of course, purely hypothetical and "never, ever" happens in my house. When I work according to a food formula, rather than using a recipe, I can scan my fridge for any usable ingredients I have on hand and quickly create something.

A quick scan of my stash shows me that I have:

- Leftover rice —**Pro Tip #1**—whenever I make rice, I always make a double batch and put the extra in my fridge or freezer
- A bag of pre-cooked chicken in my freezer—**Pro Tip #2**—I aim to always have 1-2 bags of pre-cooked chicken in the freezer for times just like this
- A bag of frozen mixed vegetables—**Pro Tip #3**—Keeping a bag of frozen mixed veggies on hand ensures we can always add veggies to any dish

I throw the chicken in a pot of hot water for a quick defrost, toss the veggies in the skillet for a few minutes, and then throw in the rice and chicken with some teriyaki sauce. For those in our family that can have eggs, they get a fried egg on top. Bam! Just like that... Chicken Fried Rice!!!

In less than 30 minutes, I have created one our family's **#savemefromtakeout** meals. I didn't need a recipe to tell me how to make this meal. I just looked at my Food Formula - looked at what I had available—and then put it together. **From panic to table in about 30 minutes**—which is conveniently the same amount of time it takes to pick up take-out. Anytime I can avoid take-out, it saves our family $25-35.

#3. IT ALLOWS ME TO RE-PURPOSE MY LEFTOVERS... THIS REDUCES MY WASTE AND SAVES ME TIME IN THE KITCHEN

We don't mind reheating a meal and having it a second time. But, any more than that, and we are not going to eat it. Previously, we found ourselves throwing away a lot of leftovers. When we decided to get our spending under control, this was one of the areas I focused on improving. Now, to avoid throwing out leftovers, I think about how to re-purpose them—not just reheat them. By thinking in terms of an equation, I can look at what I have available and turn it into a completely different meal. Then my family doesn't even know it was yesterday's meal!

If your family will not eat leftovers at all, I encourage you to think about re-purposing them in some way. Think about your food equation and see if you can take the leftovers in your fridge and turn them into a meal your family will eat.

Now, let me show you what this looks like in our home—with our Food Formula.
The plate is a visual representation of how we strive to put our meals together. From the picture, you can see how I simply choose 1-2 items from each category and mix and match them interchangeably to create a vast amount of possibilities.

RECIPE-FREE DOLLAR DINNERS

MY FOOD FORMULA
I encourage you to create your own!

SPICE

PROTEIN

VEGGIES

STARCH

FAT

Dinner FOR A DOLLAR

We apply this Formula to most any cooking style. We use it with Soup Night, Salad Night, Taco Night, Pizza Night and Loaded Baked Potato Night. We use this Food Formula to create meals using all cooking methods. In the oven, Instant Pot, crock-pot, skillet, grill, and on the stove top.

Next, you can see how we use our Food Formula to create complete meals on Skillet Night, and Loaded Baked Potato Night.

CREATE YOUR OWN
RECIPE-FREE DOLLAR DINNER
Skillet Night

CIRCLE THE ITEMS OF YOUR CHOICE TO CREATE YOUR OWN RECIPE

PROTEIN	STARCH	VEGGIES	FAT	SAUCE/SPICE
Choose 1	Choose 1	Choose 2 +	Choose 1	To Taste
Flank Steak	Corn	Kale	Olive Oil	Salt & Pepper
Pork Chop	Potato	Sweet Potatoes	Coconut Oil	Other spices
Chicken Breast	Rice	Carrots		BBQ Sauce
	Beans	Broccoli		
Ham Steak	Peas	Peppers		Sriracha
	Pasta	Onion		Teriyaki

COOKING TIPS:
- Heat your pan. Then add oil and heat your oil.
- If you're using onions & garlic, sautee for about 3 minutes
- Cook meat - If you're not familiar with cooking meat in a skillet, take time to learn! There are loads of great videos and blogs out there so you can be a pro in no time.
- Add veggies based on their cooking times.
- Add seasonings/sauces based on your family's tastes.

Baked Potato Night

CIRCLE THE ITEMS OF YOUR CHOICE TO CREATE YOUR OWN RECIPE

PROTEIN	STARCH	VEGGIES	FAT	SAUCE/SPICE
Choose 1	Choose 1	Choose 2 +	Choose 1	To Taste
Pulled Chicken	Red Potato	Roasted Tomato	Margarine	Salt & Pepper
Pulled Pork	Russet Potato	Sauteed Kale	Avocado	BBQ Sauce
Diced Ham		Sauteed Peppers		
		Sauteed Onions		
Flank Steak		Sauteed Jalapeno		
		Roasted Leeks		
		Sauteed Mushrooms		

COOKING TIPS:

- Preheat oven to 425
- Wash & dry potatoes. Rub with oil and salt and place on baking sheet
- Bake for 45 minutes
- For a quicker, hands-free option, steam potatoes in the Instant Pot. Use high pressure for 10-20 minutes depending on the size of the potato. Use a quick or natural release.
- Top with cooked toppings

You have seen my Food Formula and you have heard how using a Food Formula saves me money. Now it is time to develop your own. **Take a moment right now and think about this, if you had to ditch all the recipes and put your food values into a Food Formula that you could use to feed your family with, what would it be?** Food Values are the things that are most important to you in your food life. For me, my food values are: simple, tasty, whole food, lots of produce, allergy free, meals for $1 per person. I use these values to form all my meals.

ACTION POINT

TAKE A MOMENT TO JOT DOWN YOUR FOOD VALUES.
- What is most important to you in your food life?

NOW USE THOSE FOOD VALUES TO CREATE A FOOD FORMULA THAT YOU COULD USE TO SERVE YOUR FAMILY.

GO TO YOUR FRIDGE/FREEZER RIGHT NOW AND SEE IF THERE ARE ANY MEALS YOU CAN PUT TOGETHER IN THE NEXT DAY OR 2 USING YOUR FOOD EQUATION.

JOT DOWN A LIST OF MEALS YOUR FAMILY WOULD ENJOY USING YOUR FOOD FORMULA.

Chapter 7 – Fast-Batch Dollar Dinners

This chapter is super exciting for me to share with you, because it is my #1 planning tip for simplifying my time in the kitchen. I am definitely saving the best for last in the planning section!

Over the years, I developed a system of cooking that I now call Fast-Batch Dollar Dinners. I never set out to create it, it just slowly developed over time and evolved into my greatest time saver.

If you have heard of a capsule wardrobe, you will immediately understand Fast-Batch Dollar Dinners. The idea of a capsule wardrobe came out of the minimalist community: you purchase a few pieces of clothing that all coordinate together, so you can mix and match your items into endless amounts of combinations. The concept simplifies your purchases, your storage, your decisions, and your time. It is a way of managing your clothing, so you save time, money, and energy. This is what I do with food. I have a handful of staple ingredients I can use to create a wide variety of dishes. This process simplifies my purchases, my storage, my decisions, and my time. Just like a capsule wardrobe, it saves me time, money, and energy.

So, what the heck is the Fast-Batch Dollar Dinner system? It is where I cook an extra-large or super-sized batch of meat and re-purpose it into distinct meals throughout the week. Like the Recipe-Free Dollar Dinners shared in the last chapter, this system creates variety out of simple, core ingredients.

The system starts with volume. Specifically, doubling, tripling, or quadrupling meat when you cook.

When I quadruple a meat, we eat one portion for dinner, and then I keep the extra portions in the fridge to re-purpose over the next few days. Sometimes I cook up to eight times the amount. When I do this, we eat one portion for dinner, keep three portions in the fridge for repurposing, and then put four portions in the freezer to use another week.

Let me jump right in and show you specifically what I mean.

Let's say that on Saturday, I decide to cook an extra-large batch of ground turkey that is four times the amount I normally use for my family.

I take that ground turkey and I cook four distinct meals out of that one base ingredient. It looks like this:

	SATURDAY	SUNDAY	MONDAY
LUNCH		Taco Salad	Turkey Chili
DINNER	Taco Night	Spaghetti Squash with Marinara Meat Sauce	

An even more efficient system is if I cook a super-sized batch of ground turkey. In this example, I take seven times the amount of ground turkey I use for my family and do the above, but then take it a step further by doubling up everything I cook for dinner and serving it as leftovers the next day for lunch. When I cook seven servings of ground turkey, I can't fit that on my stove top. So, I use my giant roaster pan and put it outside, so it doesn't heat up my house. It cooks perfectly!

	SATURDAY	SUNDAY	MONDAY	TUESDAY
LUNCH		Ground Turkey Taco Leftovers	Taco Salad Leftovers	Spaghetti Squash with Marinara Meat Sauce Leftovers
DINNER	Ground Turkey Taco Night	Taco Salad	Spaghetti Squash with Marinana Meat Sauce	Taco Soup

Let's say your family doesn't eat leftovers, but you still want to cook a super-sized portion of meat and repurpose that into seven distinct meals. This isn't quite as efficient as doubling up and serving leftovers the next day, but it's still way more efficient than defrosting and cooking meat every day. That would look like this:

	SATURDAY	SUNDAY	MONDAY	TUESDAY
LUNCH		Taco Salad	Taco Soup	Chili
DINNER	Ground Turkey Taco Night	Spaghetti Squash with Marinara Meat Sauce	Shepherd's Pie	BBQ Ranch Ground Turkey Lettuce Wraps with Black Beans and Guac

When I do this, I have cooked seven distinct meals from one round of meat. I have used up the meat within three days of cooking it, so I have no challenges with food safety. By using pre-cooked meat, I have shaved off loads of time in the kitchen. By using un-frozen pre-cooked meat, I have eliminated one of the top reasons people don't cook dinner— forgetting to take something out of the freezer.

Now, even though these are quite distinct meals, it may be too much ground turkey for you in one week's time. If that's the case, here's another strategy that may work better for you. This time, you're cooking eight times the amount of ground turkey you would use for your family.

But this time, you pull out four of those portions and freeze them individually. You use the other four portions like this:

	SATURDAY	SUNDAY	MONDAY
LUNCH		Taco Salad	Taco Soup
DINNER	Ground Turkey Taco Night	Spaghetti Squash with Marinara Meat Sauce	

OR like this:

	SATURDAY	SUNDAY	MONDAY
LUNCH		Taco Leftovers	Spaghetti Squash with Marinara Meat Sauce Leftovers
DINNER	Ground Turkey Taco Night (double portion)	Spaghetti Squash with Marinara Meat Sauce (double portion)	

Then, on Monday or Tuesday, you go to your freezer and pull out four portions of a different meat that you cooked last week. You then follow this same system and prepare four distinct meals from that meat.

As I've been studying my own food budget for several years, I've found that I can serve my family a hot lunch for less than I can serve them a cold one. Because of this, my favorite system from above is to double up at dinner and serve leftovers for lunch. To me, this is the ultimate plan for saving time, money, and energy. Sometimes, this gets a little old, so I just mix it up so that it keeps working for us.

I showed you how the Fast-Batch Dollar Dinner system works with the simple, humble ingredient of ground turkey. I showed you how I mix and match the ingredients from my food equation to make simple meals with the littlest amount of effort possible.

If this concept seems mind-blowing to you, I have great news!! Ground turkey is not the only meat I do this with! I literally do it with all my meats:

- **Ham**
- **Pork Roast**
- **Whole Chickens**
- **Salsa Chicken**
- **Chicken Breasts**

*We have a beef allergy in our home, so we consume very little beef. I don't actually do Fast-Batch Dollar Dinners with beef, but if you eat beef, you definitely can!!!! Fast Batch Dollar Dinners will work with beef roasts, ground beef, steaks, flank steaks, and stew meat.

ACTION POINT

IF YOU HAVE 15 MINUTES RIGHT NOW, THINK ABOUT THE MEAT YOUR FAMILY MOST OFTEN CONSUMES:

THINK ABOUT 2-4-6-8 DISTINCT MEALS THAT YOU KNOW YOUR FAMILY LIKES, THAT YOU CAN MAKE WITH THIS MEAT:

1.
2.
3.
4.
5.
6.
7.
8.

IF YOU HAVE EXTRA TIME RIGHT NOW, THINK ABOUT OTHER TYPES OF MEAT YOUR FAMILY CONSUMES AND LIST OUT MEALS THAT YOU CAN MAKE WITH THESE.

Part 4: Shopping Stage

Chapter 8 – Buy at the Best Price

To reduce your food bill by the maximum amount, you'll need to buy your food at the best price in your area. It's possible to reduce your bill dramatically by skipping this step and just following the other steps, but if you want to reduce your food bill by the largest amount possible, while still honoring your food values and keeping things simple, you'll have to take some time and focus heavily on this step.

This is the most time-consuming step, so if your schedule is slammed right now, I recommend skipping this step and coming back later, when you have more time and energy.

If your goals necessitate that you slash your food budget to the lowest possible point, I encourage you to focus heavily here. Carve some time out in your schedule. For a short amount of time, treat it like a small, part-time job. The time you invest in this step now can yield savings for years to come. I can tell you, with certainty, that the time I have spent on this in the past has paid me handsomely. The yield has been exponentially more than the time I have put into it. I would have to work 12.5 hours a week at a $20/hour job to yield the $1000/month I've saved our family by changing our food habits. There is NO WAY that I spend 12.5 hours more per week saving money on my food bill. In fact, now that I am through the research stage, I spend less time thinking about, shopping for, and preparing food than I did before. So, a little investment on the front end really is worth it on the back end – I promise! Stick with me! So, let's dive in...

To buy your food at the best prices, you need to know what the best prices are in your area. To find out what the best prices are, you're going to have to do some research. The bad news is that this takes some time.

The good news is, you don't have to keep doing it. This is a one-time effort. And then, after that, unless something really changes with your food values, you just need to occasionally check in to make sure that you're still getting your food for the lowest cost in your area.

When I got to the "find the best prices for my food" stage, I carved out some time in my schedule as an appointment in my calendar. I talked to my husband and let him know that I needed some time without any kids to think, research, and price shop. I put this time on our calendar and made sure that he was available to take care of the kids, so I had the time I needed to concentrate. There is strong research to suggest that multi-tasking is not efficient. Obviously, as mothers, we have to multi-task a lot. But when it's time to do something of value, we need to set that aside and focus on the task at hand, to yield the best results.

STEP 1 – SIT DOWN AND RECORD HOW YOU REALLY EAT.

Take a moment and jot down the building blocks of your family's diet – this will help you figure out what you need to price check.

For our family, we eat the following items:

- Meat
- Veggies
- Fruits
- Fats
- Starches
- Allergen-free Substitutes

You'll have some variation from your building blocks here and there, but probably not a lot. Most people consistently work with the same building blocks for their food plans.

STEP 2 – DETERMINE WHICH CATEGORIES ARE MOST EXPENSIVE AND FOCUS ON THOSE FIRST.

Look at your list and determine which components of your diet are the most expensive and have the widest variations in pricing. Also, look at the components that have relatively steady prices. You will want to focus on locating the best pricing on the items that are the most expensive and have the widest variation in pricing.

If you look at the list of food that we eat, meat is both the most expensive component of that diet AND has the widest variation in pricing—followed by vegetables, and then fruit. Whole food starch prices are relatively steady; I simply don't see wide pricing variations on whole rice, beans, potatoes, or corn.

So, the first thing I did was find the very best pricing in our area for the meats that we eat. Then I focused on the best pricing for produce. And, finally, the best pricing for occasional allergen-free foods. After a while, I also paid loose attention to finding the best prices on whole food starches.

When first getting started, you will want to focus on the areas that are the most expensive AND have the widest variations in pricing. Foods in that category will give you the biggest return on your time investment—lowering your food budget by the most dollars in the least amount of time.

ACTION POINT

NOW IT'S YOUR TURN:

In order of expense, what components of your diet are the most expensive?

1.
2.
3.
4.

While you are getting started, I recommend that you focus on finding the best prices for the top 1-3 most expensive components of your diet. Of course, if you have another way you want to do this, go for it! Just jot it down here.

STEP 3 – DEVELOP THE RIGHT MENTALITY AROUND FOOD SAVINGS.

Mentality is a big deal.

Back when I was spending $1200 a month on groceries, I bought things whenever I needed them or wanted them, with absolutely no thought of waiting for them to go on sale. If I wanted to make chili, I would put a can of beans on my grocery list, go to the store, see them for $1, and put two in my cart without even thinking about the price. When they would go on sale for $0.80/can, I wouldn't even consider buying extra, because I legitimately didn't think that saving $0.20 on a can of beans was worth my effort.

Anyone else like this? Think that saving $0.20 on a can of beans is not worth your effort? Girl, I have been there.

What about this...

Think about those beans. Imagine that you never, ever paid full price for those beans again. Imagine that you waited until they were $0.80/can and *only* ever bought them at that price. When you saw them for $0.80/can, you stocked up, so that the next time you wanted to make chili, you already had beans on the shelf, and you wouldn't have to pay $1/can when you got the craving.

Still doesn't seem like a big deal, does it?

$0.80 vs. $1 for beans represents a 20% savings. I'm not great at math, but I got that one for sure.

Now, what if all your groceries could follow this same pattern?

All of them have an everyday price. In this case, $1/unit for the beans.

All of them have a sale price. In this case, $0.80/unit for the beans.

What if I told you that all your groceries can be purchased for a 20% savings if you are patient and only buy them on sale. So, let's say that before you picked up this book, you were spending $1000/month on groceries. By simply focusing on only ever buying food when it's for sale at 20% off, you will reduce your bill by $200/month. That's substantial. Makes you re-think the $0.80 can of beans, doesn't it? It's not such a humble discount after all!

Let's take it a step further. Did you know that, in our area, a few times a year, canned beans go on a fire sale for about $0.50/can? That's not just a $0.50/can savings, that's a 50% savings!

Now, imagine that you waited until canned beans went down to their fire sale price of $0.50/can and you *only* ever bought them when they were $0.50/can. Imagine that you bought as many canned beans at the fire sale price as you could use and safely store for 3-6 months. You never paid regular price, and you tried hard never even to pay sale price. You held out for fire sale pricing only. You will have saved 50% on your beans over the course of a year. Makes you tilt your head a bit, but I doubt anyone would go crazy over saving $0.50 on a can of beans.

More importantly, now imagine that you did this with all your food. Did you know that almost everything you consume goes on a fire sale at some point in time during the year? In my experience, this generally happens 2-3 times a year. What if you focused on trying to only buy your food when it was at fire sale prices?

If you waited for fire sale prices and bought as much as you could use and safely store for 3-6 months' time, you could potentially save 50% off your food bill. Makes you re-think the $0.50 can of beans, doesn't it?

Could your mind handle it if I said it gets better? Did you know that if you learn to cook dried beans, that same serving of beans goes from $1/can to $0.25/can when bought at everyday pricing? $0.25 a can is a 75% savings on regular-priced canned beans!

This 75% savings example is not available for every ingredient you buy, but it IS a good representation of the type of savings you can realize on your ingredients if you are willing and able to spend more time on food preparation. Imagine being able to save 75% on your food costs on more than just this one item.

These fire sale prices won't do you much good for routine, perishable staples for your family that must be purchased every trip—like butter, milk, eggs—but they CAN apply to things that can be purchased most anytime and stored for when you need them.

NOTE: Food prices vary wildly by region. You all may be looking at the can of beans analogy and thinking "I wish!" Maybe your everyday price is $2. Your sale price is $1.49 and your fire sale price is $1. The principle will apply anywhere. Focus on the percentages and per-unit pricing available in your area. If you are living in Alaska, Hawaii, or California, you may not be able to get down to $1 per person per meal like I can here with low-ish food prices, but you can still utilize this concept—if you focus on percentages—and focus on some food price rules.

I SEE GROCERIES AVAILABLE AT FOUR PRICING LEVELS:

1. **Overpriced (think boutique or expensive stores)**
2. **Regular, everyday good price**
3. **Sale price**
4. **Fire sale price (This is the price where the store feels like you stole it from them. Also called a loss leader.)**

HERE ARE MY CARDINAL RULES OF FOOD PRICING:

1. Never pay full price.
2. If you need it and it's on sale, buy a month's worth.
3. When it's on a fire sale, buy as much as you can use and safely store for 3-6 months.

If you want to minimize your grocery bill as much as possible, write these down somewhere. Commit them to memory. Make them your own personal shopping policy.

At this point, you may be worried that my food storage is outrageously out of control. You may envision me with rations stored under my children's beds or disaster shelter-type storage. I promise you it's not like that at all. No bunkers here!!!! We have a very normal-sized pantry situation.

We do, however, have an extra freezer and an extra fridge. Personally, I couldn't shop every two weeks for a family our size without both the extra fridge and freezer. If your family is not as large as ours, or if you shop one time a week, you can get by without the fridge. However, I would say that anyone who eats meat and wants to buy their meat at the lowest price possible, will need an extra freezer. I don't think you can consume meat, buy it at the best prices of the year, and not have a freezer. Where I live, these can be purchased inexpensively in the used market and do not cost much extra in electricity usage.

ACTION POINT

WRITE THE CARDINAL RULES OF FOOD PRICING DOWN SOMEWHERE PROMINENT.

CONSIDER IF IT MAKES SENSE FOR YOU TO GET A SPARE FREEZER.
If so, think about how you can save up for a spare freezer. If you are married, include your spouse in this conversation.

STEP 4 – FIGURE OUT WHAT THE REGULAR, SALE, AND FIRE SALE PRICES ARE ON YOUR MOST FREQUENTLY PURCHASED ITEMS.

You know the cardinal rules: never buy at full price and buy at fire sale pricing whenever you can. But how do you know what the regular price, the sale price, and the fire sale price are on the food you buy?

The most thorough and accurate way to know is to have a price book. Put simply, this is a place for you to record the prices of the items you purchased, when you purchased them, and from where. When you keep track of this long enough, you will start to see the pricing trends. This will turn you into the most conscientious food consumer in the city. Which is awesome. Seriously.

You may be thinking there is no way you're carrying around a food price sheet and recording your prices over the course of the year! You thought this was supposed to be simple!

I feel you. We are kindred spirits. That's exactly what I thought when I read about price books. That is why I personally didn't do one. I am just not that organized. If you are, awesome! Go for it! And if you aren't, that's okay, too. So, what's the alternative for those of us who are too lazy... *ahem*...busy...to use a price sheet year-round?

You have a few options:

1. CHEAT OFF YOUR FRIENDS' PAPER.

Seriously. This is one of the strategies that I used when I first got started. Facebook is perfect for cheating off our friends' papers. Jump on Facebook and ask your local friends, "Where are the cheapest places to buy produce? To buy meat? To buy allergen-free products?" If you only buy grass-fed products, ask around for the best places to buy grass-fed products. Post it on your page—post it in mommy groups—post it in any specialty food groups that you may be a part of. In addition to this, I recommend that you think of your most frugal friends and shoot them a message. Ask them where they find the best places to buy at the best prices. This is a fantastic strategy—a real time saver.

2. TAKE YOUR PRICE BOOK AND AN AFTERNOON.

This is the speed dating version of the price book suggestion listed above. You can take the price book and, in one afternoon, list out all the staple ingredients that your family consumes on a regular basis. Go around to several local grocery stores in your immediate area and record prices on all your staple items. Compare them overall. See if you can find one store that, when you consider all your items, rises above all the others. Start here, by making this your Main Store. The problem with the speed dating version is that prices do vary, so you won't be able to tell if this grocery store is always cheaper overall than your other options. But it does give you a good starting point. When you cheat and take this short cut, know that you may need to pay closer attention and revise as you go.

3. CHOOSE THE GROCERY STORE IN YOUR LOCAL AREA KNOWN TO HAVE THE BEST OVERALL PRICES AND JUST START THERE.

Here is an article highlighting what others have said are the chains known for having the best prices. Check this out to see if you have any of these thrifty-minded chains in your local area.
https://clark.com/shopping-retail/cheapest-grocery-stores/

ACTION POINT

IF YOU HAVE 10 MINUTES
Post on Facebook or send a text to local friends to find out where the cheapest sources of your staples are. Find the stores with the best overall prices.

IF YOU HAVE 15 MINUTES
Decide how you are going to do some pricing research.
- Are you going to keep a thorough pricing sheet?
- Are you going to set aside an afternoon to do some store comparisons?

- Are you going to cheat off a friend's paper?
- Are you going to go with the most economical chain available?

NOW, TAKE A MOMENT AND PUT YOUR ACTION STEP INTO YOUR CALENDAR.

If you are taking an afternoon to price compare, put it in the calendar and line up childcare.

STEP 5 — LEARN TO TAKE ADVANTAGE OF SEASONAL TRENDS.

After you have done this for a while, you will start to see the seasonal trends. Certain things are on sale every fall, winter, spring, and summer. Certain things go on sale around every major holiday. If you can capitalize on these trends, you will save money.

In general, prices on groceries tend to drop as demand rises. So, if you think of things that are popular in certain seasons—like baking in the fall and grilling in the summer—you will generally be able to predict some seasonal trends in pricing. This isn't an exact science, but it will give you a good idea.

One of my favorite things is to stock up on holiday favorites *after* the holiday. A good example of this is when I purchased 16 packages of corned beef for $0.75/pound after St. Patrick's Day. This forced me to get creative with corned beef, and I have now learned several new ways to prepare it. You can do this by stocking up on ham after Christmas and Easter, turkeys after Thanksgiving, or ribs and hot dogs after summer holidays.

STEP 6 – SET ASIDE A PORTION OF YOUR MONTHLY BILL FOR STOCKING UP.

I set aside a portion of my monthly bill for stocking up on things when they are at fire sale pricing. I try really hard to only buy my meat when it's at 'Drive It Like You Stole It' pricing. In order to do that, I have to have money freed up in my monthly budget for me to spontaneously buy four hams when they hit $0.79 a pound, or 12 trays of boneless, skinless chicken breasts when they hit $0.79 cents a pound. (Actual prices I paid this year for meat.)

Now, before you say, "Oh my gosh, we never have meat prices like that in my city," let me say this—you may very well never have meat prices like that in your city, truly. But if I surveyed 100 people in my city, at least 95 of them would say, "Oh my gosh, we never have meat prices like that in my city." But we do. So, this is the part where you have to be patient and prepared. And when it strikes, you buy as much as you can use and store safely for 3-6 months.

When you first start doing this, your freezer is going to be seriously lacking in meat variety. But if you stick with it, over time, as you pick up more meat at fire sale pricing, your freezer *will* eventually gain variety.

STEP 7 – LEARN TO CAPITALIZE ON LOSS LEADERS, WITHOUT TAKING THE BAIT.

"Loss leaders" are items that a grocery store has put on sale at a loss to them, in an effort to lure you into the store, so you will buy things that are not on sale. If you can learn to capitalize on these loss leaders *without* taking the bait and buying other things at regular price, you will have a simple source of savings without having to work hard to investigate good deals.

It is relatively easy to identify loss leaders without even knowing your pricing very well. In general, if your grocery store has a limit of one, two, or four per customer on an item, it's a great sale, and you can feel good about picking up the maximum amount. Are they at a fire sale price? Maybe not. But they're at least a strong sale.

Another great indicator is if it is on the front page of the store ad. In general, their best prices are on the front page. If I am in a hurry, I will often only look at the front of the flyers for my best source of sales for the week.

How do you capitalize on loss leaders without taking the bait and buying other things while you are there?

Shop at your best store for your regular trip. On my grocery planning pages, I jot down all the relevant loss leaders on my shopping page. As I am shopping at my main store, I compare the prices here against the loss leaders from other stores. If the loss leaders at the other stores are enough of a savings for me to warrant an additional stop, I will hold off on them and grab them at the other store on my way home.

As mentioned previously, I limit all my shopping to one day every two weeks. So, I factor in the time and energy of stopping at another store when I am deciding if it is worth the trip. For me, and I am sure for many of you, it is not exclusively about best prices. I must balance finding the best price against the time and energy that I have available. So, sometimes I make a separate trip to grab these loss leaders, and sometimes I don't.

STEP 8 – FIND THE BEST DAYS OF THE WEEK TO SHOP AT MY STORES.

Find out if any of your local stores offer stronger sales on a certain day of the week.

Sprouts Grocery Store is the best example of this. They have Double Ad Day on Wednesday. This is where they have items from both lasts week's flyer and the next week's flyer on sale at the same time. You are effectively getting twice as many items on sale as any other day of the week. If you shop at Sprouts, you should try to only go on Wednesdays.

ACTION POINT

FIND OUT IF ANY OF YOUR LOCAL GROCERY STORES HAVE DAYS OF THE WEEK WITH STRONGER SALES.

Chapter 9 – Saving Money on Shopping Day

You have done all the work to set your budget... you did a complete inventory and made a meal plan... you pulled out your cash and assembled your clipboard. Great work! Now it is shopping day! It's important that you are just as intentional with your habits on shopping day as with the behaviors leading up to it. If you lose your focus on shopping day, while you are in the store, you could end up blowing your budget and negate all the effort you have put in so far.

Over the years, I have noticed several important strategies to help me save money at the store:

Eat before you shop.
I know you know this. But it is so important that it's worth stating at the top of this list. Do not go grocery shopping when hungry! Do whatever you need to do to eat before you shop! Even if you can't get a full meal in, a small snack in the car will at least take the edge off.

Bring water.
A lot of times when we think we're hungry, we're actually thirsty. Drinking water is a great way to stave off hunger and cravings.

Bring your clipboard.
Your clipboard has your shopping list, the loss leaders at other stores, your meal plan, your inventory list, and your pricing notebook (if you are keeping one).

Bring your cash.
If you find it difficult to stick to your cash budget and not overspend, leave your cards at home.

Don't go to the store in a hurry.
The way you plan, shop, and cook for your family can save your family thousands of dollars a year. In my case, changing my habits saved me $12,000 a year!!! This is substantial and worthy of your time. Not that you need to spend all day at the store, but it will take time and attention at the store to yield maximum savings. You will be developing new habits of price checking—this takes some extra time, especially at first. You will get faster over time. But even for me, years later, I still make it an intentional decision not to go to the store in a hurry. It is a worthy effort and deserving of my time and attention. I bring my business mindset with me. For me, this is my greatest financial contribution to my family.

Don't go to the store when angry, anxious, or depressed.
If you are having a really bad day, skip the store and reschedule for another day. If you are having a lot of bad days, reach out to someone. Find a trusted friend or professional. Shopping and strong negative emotions are not a great combo.

Do whatever you can to leave your kids and your husband at home.
I know this may be inconvenient, but statistically, you will spend more when you bring them along. If you must bring them along, brainstorm (ahead of time) strategies for not allowing your kids or spouse to influence your shopping. Make a plan for that and train your kids about your expectations.

Stick to your list! Except for fire sale pricing, don't deviate from the list!!!
You worked hard on this list. It's exactly what you need. Trust it. Don't let the grocery store win by tricking you into buying what you don't need or didn't plan on. As I stated in the previous chapter, I set aside about 20% of my food budget for stocking up on items at fire sale prices. My

experience is that fire sale pricing is often not advertised. I can't predict these sales, so I need to be prepared when they come my way, without being tricked into adding other items.

Bring your big girl panties.
I love to bless my family with good food. Sometimes it's hard for me not to be able to buy them all the good food they would love to eat. Heck, sometimes it's hard for me not to be able to buy myself all the good food that I want to eat!!! But I need to keep my eyes and mind on what my end goals are. I don't want to eat our retirement ever again. Imagine never being able to retire with dignity, because you wanted to buy all the food you loved at the grocery store. Seems kinda silly when you put it this way, right?

Before you go to the store, remind yourself what your goals are. Hold tight to what you are trying to accomplish. Keep that in your mind, put on your big girl panties, and start your shopping. It begins and ends with a strong mindset. You can do this. Your hard work and discipline can help your family succeed financially.

ACTION POINT

• Take 10 minutes and jot down some habits you could improve on shopping day to help you hit your grocery budget goals.

• Take 5 minutes to remind yourself of your why. Why are you making these changes? What are you hoping to achieve?

Part 5:
Kitchen Plan

Ch. 10 - Reduce Waste

This might be my most obvious step yet... but here goes nothing....

One way to reduce your grocery bill is to stop throwing away food.

The average American throws away 25% of the food and drinks they buy—averaging $1,600 per year. That's $133 of food, per month, thrown in the trash. (nrdc.org)

Stop and consider that: $133 per month. **Thrown in the trash**. If you took no other tips from this book and exclusively eliminated your food waste, you would—on average—lower your bill by $133 a month—and simultaneously improve the environment.

Seriously. This is staggering to me.

Take a moment right now and think about how much food you throw away each week.

It might be hard to admit it. I know it was particularly hard for me to face. Once I was honest with myself, I realized we were throwing away a lot of food every single week. I am confident we were at or over the national average. Uncooked meat that I never got around to preparing, cooked meat that I didn't repurpose into another dish, uneaten leftovers, and loads of forgotten produce.

When I started to think of food in terms of dollar bills, I realized that every time I threw away a bunch of brown bananas, I was throwing away $1. Every time I threw away a tray of uncooked chicken, I threw away a $5 or $10 bill. Every time I threw away uneaten leftovers, I threw away a $5 or $10 bill. And, to make it worse, if we had chosen to eat out—instead of cooking the food we already had at home—it quadrupled our financial waste. Not only did we spend $25-$40 on eating out, but we didn't cook what we had and ended up throwing it in the trash. So, I could be looking at a true cost of $30-$50 when we chose take-out over home cooking. Talk about paying for food twice.

I also had to realize that not only is throwing out food a total waste of money, it is really disrespectful.

In our home, my husband works full-time, and I stay home with the monkeys. When I throw away food, I am disrespecting my husband and the work he has done to pay for that food. Think of food in terms of hours worked to earn it. If he earns $20/hour, and I throw away $5 of food, with taxes, he probably had to work for 20 minutes to pay for that food... in the trash. Ugh! So, by failing to make a plan, I just threw away 20 minutes of my husband's life. When I thought of it this way, I felt pretty motivated to change.

When I throw away food, I am disrespecting myself and the time I have spent thinking about, shopping for, and preparing it. All this work I put in to plan my food, shop for it, and buy it at the best prices. That's quite a bit of energy spent to just turn around and throw 25% of it away.

When I throw away food, I am disrespecting the farmer who grew that food and the picker who picked it. Stop for a moment and think of all the people that had to work to get those grapes into your fridge. Someone started a farm, planted those grapes, harvested them, packed them. Someone started a transportation company and transported them. Someone started a grocery store, unpacked them, displayed them, answered your questions, rang you up, bagged them and helped you to your car. That's easily 13 different people that brought you your grapes. When I throw them in the trash because I forgot to wash them and put them in a place where my children can see them, I show them that I do not value their effort and energy.
When I throw away food, I am also disrespecting the planet. Until re-

cently, I had ZERO awareness of the environmental impact of food waste. But it is actually a big problem.

One-third of all the food produced for human consumption never makes it to the consumer—resulting in a tremendous amount of greenhouse gasses. If food waste were a country, it would represent the 3rd largest contributor to greenhouse gas emissions—behind China and the U.S. **Reducing worldwide food waste could make critical changes to the environment.**

http://www.fao.org/fileadmin/templates/nr/sustainability_pathways/docs/FWF_and_climate_change.pdf

There is just no good excuse for throwing away food. For me, it simply represented poor planning and sometimes downright laziness. Something which I was, with a little bit of effort, able to drastically reduce.

When I got serious about reducing my food waste, I first had to contemplate what factors led me to waste food in the first place, so I could change my habits.

Let's talk about the big reasons I realized we were wasting large amounts of food each week.

#1 REASON FOR FOOD WASTE - OVER-BUYING

Right? Buying too much is a recipe for food waste. If you buy more than you can eat or can safely store, you will waste food. For me, there were a lot of reasons why I bought too much food.

1. I WAS NOT REALISTIC ABOUT OUR CURRENT FOOD HABITS.

I was famous for this one. Maybe you are, too. There are times that we do a lot of juicing. Juicing helps us when our systems get out of whack and we need a reset. When we are juicing, we need profound amounts of produce. Unnatural amounts. During these times, I buy our produce directly from a wholesaler in case quantities. This works amazingly when we are juicing. When we're not, it's a terrible plan. So, if we aren't juicing, I have concluded that, for the most part, I should not buy from the wholesaler—no matter how good the deal is. There are exceptions, but I have made a mental note to be super careful about this.

This doesn't just happen at the wholesale—it also happens at the regular grocery store. Eating a lot of fruits and veggies is a strong food value for us. Sometimes, in the store, I get so excited about eating lots of fruits and vegetables that I buy more than we can eat or safely store before the food will spoil. You will remember from a previous chapter that one way that I combat this is to quantify items on my grocery list.

Moral of this story—be realistic about your current food habits. Do not buy what you *want* your food habits to be—you must buy for what they *actually* are.

2. I WAS NOT REALISTIC ABOUT MY TIME OR ENERGY FOR THAT PERIOD.

You've figured out by now that I work really hard to balance the resources of money, time and energy. Sometimes in my life, I have extra time and energy. When I have that, I can buy fussier foods. Foods that might need more time or energy to process.

For instance, let's say that I have access to 80 pounds of strawberries for $25. (This just happened this week.) I think we can all agree that $0.31/pound for strawberries is a *fire sale* price. I had to turn it down because I am writing this week, and I don't have time to process 80 pounds of strawberries. Our family can't eat 80 pounds of strawberries before they spoil. In the past, I would have gone and gotten it because it was such a good deal! We would have eaten 30 pounds of it, and then 50 pounds of it would have spoiled. In this case, I would have paid about $0.83 cents per pound for the strawberries that we actually consumed. $0.83/pound is a good price for strawberries in my area, but not a fire sale price, so it's not worth an extra trip for me. And had I not found a way to safely store it or give it away, it would have resulted in about 50 pounds of food waste. It didn't make sense for me, this week, when I didn't have extra time or energy, to go buy those strawberries. In this case, I weighed the time, money, and energy and concluded it wasn't a good deal for me this week.

This may be true for you in different ways. Maybe you don't have the energy to cook dried beans and freeze them for later use. If you're not honest about your energy levels, you will buy the dried beans, and they will sit in your panty—money wasted—taking up space— and nag at you every time you see them. If this is the case, your best value is buying canned beans at fire sale prices and passing on the dried beans. It isn't just about buying food at the cheapest possible prices, it's about buying food *that you will use* at the cheapest possible prices.

I have already shared with you that part of my planning process involves looking at my calendar for the two-week time period that I am shopping for. If we have an especially busy time period, I know that I need to plan for extremely simple food. Or maybe I need to spend more and buy some convenience-type items. Though these types of items cost more at the store than my traditional Dinner for a Dollar meals, these key choices at the store will save me from getting take-out later in the week.

Moral of this story—be realistic about the time and energy that you have available during that time period – and plan accordingly. No matter how cheap it is, it's not a good deal if you can't use it.

3. I WENT TO THE STORE WITHOUT A PLAN.

This is big. I have already covered this in Chapter 4. But, it's worth repeating here because it directly relates to food waste. Do not go to the store without a plan—it can easily lead to buying food that you will not get around to preparing.

Even if you can't do a full-scale plan like I covered earlier, at least sit in the parking lot before you go in and sketch out a quick plan. Think about what you need and how much of it you need. Then jot it down. With proper planning, your spontaneous trips will be reduced dramatically. But let's face it, they're still going to happen. So, just because you don't have time to do a full-scale plan does not mean you go into the store with no plan at all. At least make an itty-bitty one. Taking even that snippet of time in the car will save you money at the register and reduce the amount of food that ends up in the trash.

#2 REASON FOR FOOD WASTE – NOT COOKING THE FOOD I BUY

I'm going to be honest here. This was the main contributor to food waste for me. I just simply didn't prepare the food that I purchased. There were a lot of factors that contributed to this —planning too many overly complicated meals, laziness, poor planning, distraction. There are no tricks here that helped me overcome this. It was just a decision. Just me + my big girl panties. This is where the will to have a different financial future kicked in for me. **Somewhere along the way, I realized that the single most powerful way I could improve our finances was to cook food every night.** Nothing else destroys our budget more than eating out. So, when I don't want to prepare the food I have in the fridge, I just have to give myself the big girl panty talk and remind myself that, though it seems like a small decision right now (to cook the chicken in my fridge or get take-out), it's really a financially critical decision.

If I can do it, you can too. Pull out your big girl panties and dust them off. If you don't have a pair, stop right now and go buy them. In order to have a different financial future for your family, you are going to need them.

One word on fruit for snacks. Sadly, my kids eat infinitely more fruit and veggies for snacks when I prepare it for them. I know that preparing fruit ahead of time reduces the shelf life, so this is a delicate balance. But grapes that are washed and out of the grape bag have a 1,000% greater chance of being eaten in my house. (No research here, just making up a number that's probably accurate—ha!) If you know you hate to peel mangoes, or hate to wash grapes, or hate to cut a watermelon, be honest about this and don't buy them. It doesn't matter how much your little snowflakes love watermelon. If there isn't someone there who is actually going to "cut" the watermelon, you will eventually throw it in the trash, and buying it has been a waste.

Cook the chicken. Chop the veggies. Cut the fruit. Big girl panties.

It really is that simple.

#3 REASON FOR FOOD WASTE – NOT EATING OUR LEFTOVERS

I don't really have a problem with leftovers, and my family certainly will eat them, but no one really enjoys them very much. We typically will eat them one time. After that, they need to be repurposed or they will end up in the trash. You saw in my chapter on Recipe-Free Dollar Dinners how easily you can use your food formula to repurpose ingredients in your fridge — turning them into an entirely different meal. Repurposing leftovers saves me time, money, and energy, all while reducing my food waste. If you regularly find yourself throwing away leftovers, re-read the chapter on Recipe-Free Dollar Dinners and see if you can utilize that strategy to reduce waste.

Hot tip alert

Every few days, take a quick scan of your fridge and see what you need to use up.

Ask yourself, what can I do with this? How can I re-purpose it? The simple act of asking yourself this question, engaging your creative problem-solving juices, will help you reduce your waste.

This habit of checking in every few days has a profound effect on reducing our waste. Many times, I am shocked to discover that, every few days, I have enough to serve everyone lunch. Bonus!!!

4 REASON FOR FOOD WASTE – CONCERN OVER FOOD SAFETY

Let's switch gears here and talk about food safety. By this point, you are probably starting to think seriously about how to reduce your waste. But, if you're like me, you're probably wondering, "How do I know if my food is safe? I don't want to make my family sick."

"When in doubt, throw it out" is one of my cardinal rules in the kitchen. I have ZERO interest in making my family sick to save $5. Obviously. And I'm sure you feel exactly the same way I do. So, know that I am *not* talking about feeding your family risky food in order to save money. I'm talking about planning, to keep your food from getting to the danger zone in the first place.

So, how do you know how long you can safely keep food?
I'm not an expert here, so I am going to share what the experts have to say about this.

Here is an incredible resource on food safety—from shopping, to handling, to thawing, to prep, to freezing and storage. I recommend that if you want to learn more about food safety, you check it out on the Food Safety and Inspection Service site here:

https://www.fsis.usda.gov/wps/portal/fsis/topics/food-safety-education.

You can find their recommendations on how long food can be safely stored in our Appendix.

Additionally, there's a free app called the Food Keeper App, put out by the USDA. It tells you the shelf life of all the major foods you would want to cook with AND allows you to set a reminder on your calendar of when the food needs to be used by. Bonus! The app also notifies you whenever there have been food or beverage recalls—which I really appreciate. I am a low app user, but I actually use this app.

I'm not sure if you can relate to this or not, but many times I throw food away simply because I *cannot* remember when I prepared it. How can I forget something I just made three days ago? I have no idea—but I do. So, in the trash it goes... so wasteful. To combat this, I have started marking the containers in my fridge, so I know exactly when I prepared them. In addition to using the Food Keeper App to remind you when you need to throw your food away, you can also use food prep stickers to mark when you prepared a dish so you know when it needs to be thown out by.

#5 REASON FOR FOOD WASTE — DISORGANIZED FOOD STORAGE SPACES

Having a *moderately* organized fridge, freezer, and pantry WILL help you reduce your food waste. I'm not talking about Pinterest modeling here. So, get that crazy talk outta your head. Ain't nobody got time for that. I am talking about your spaces being functional—where you can see and access everything easily.

When you can't see or access your food easily, you will waste more food. From here forward, remember that you will be doing a full inventory of your fridge, freezer, and pantry before every shopping day, so over time, your spaces will naturally get better organized.

ACTION POINT

TO REDUCE FOOD WASTE, WE ARE GOING TO START BY GETTING SOME
BASIC ORGANIZATION INTO YOUR FOOD STORAGE SPACES.

IF YOU HAVE 5 MINUTES: TACKLE YOUR FRIDGE.
- Set a timer for 5 minutes.
- Go to your fridge and throw out anything that's gone bad.
- hrow out anything you're not sure is bad or not.
- Look for anything that needs to be used in the next 1-3 days and make a mental plan for it.
- If your refrigerator needs a full clean-out (whose doesn't?!), schedule an hour to do a full cleaning, and put it on your calendar.

IF YOU HAVE 15 MINUTES, QUICKLY TACKLE YOUR FREEZER.
- Set a timer for 15 minutes.
- Go to your freezer.
- Throw out anything that is freezer burnt.
- Look up recipes for how to use up those frozen collard greens, or deer sausage, or cranberries – add these meals to your next meal plan.
- Set to the side anything that you feel like your family will not eat and make a plan for it.
- If you cannot find a use for something, send a message to friends and family to see if anyone will use it.
- Quickly re-organize your freezer to make it easier for you to see and access your foods.

Chapter 11 - Saving You Minutes to Save You Dollars

Finding ways to save time in the kitchen is a critical way I have reduced my food costs. The more I simplify my time in the kitchen, the more meals we eat at home. The more meals we eat at home, the less we get take-out. Show me the money.

I have already shared with you my two biggest time hacks in previous chapters—Recipe-Free Dollar Dinners and Fast-Batch Dollar Dinners. These are my biggies!!!!! But I have a few more time savers up my sleeve that I want to share with you. I hope they help you as much as they have helped me.

PREP HACK #1 - ENLIST SOME HELP WHENEVER YOU CAN – MARTYRDOM IS NOT A BADGE OF MOTHERHOOD

Some of you may not have this luxury. Maybe you have four kids under the age of 5, your husband is a deep-sea welder who is gone for one month at a time, you're new to the area, and you live 2,000 miles from family. You probably need to do all your food prep yourself.

But most of us have some help available to us—we're just not utilizing it. Maybe you can swap with a friend. Maybe you can have your mom come help. If you're married, maybe your spouse can chip in. But... I am going to say that your greatest source of kitchen help is learning to utilize your ankle biters.

There are a lot of memes about moms that won't ask for help because their kids don't do it right, because it's easier to do it yourself, or because you don't want to deal with the attitude. If I could shout one more thing at you in this book, this would be it. Plug your ears if you don't want to hear it. Here it goes...don't say I didn't warn you.

"GET YOUR KIDS INVOLVED IN THE KITCHEN!!!!!!"

Seriously. As early as you can. Not even kidding. This will take time in the beginning. Which is so hard... I know. But trust me when I say this: the investment of time that you put in on the front end, training your kids in the kitchen, will MORE THAN pay for itself on the back end.

My kids are now 17, 15, 8, and 5. My 17- and 15-year-olds can do anything in the kitchen. They can use my pressure cookers. They can cook a whole chicken. They know how to make bone broth and cook dried beans. They can make pancakes from scratch, bake cakes from scratch (one of them can). They can make umpteen kinds of salad and can roast vegetables.

This didn't happen overnight. This happened over a lifetime spent in the kitchen, beside their mother, pitching in. So, not only are they great helpers for me and great workers for others, more importantly, they are prepared for their own food life outside of our home. They know how to shop on a budget and how to cook on a budget. I am very happy that I took the time to teach them. I am happy that I dealt with the spills, the broken glasses, the carrots dropped in the trash (probably many dozens over the years). Lest you read this and think I am a perfect parent (or think I think I am a perfect parent), know this— my kids are wild monkeys half the time and my house is messier than it should be all the time. But this is one thing I did well, so I am sharing it with you now. I taught them how to run a kitchen, and you can teach yours, too.

Obviously, you need to evaluate what your children can safely do to help, and balance that with your ability to tolerate your children helping you in the kitchen. I recommend stretching your capacity to tolerating your kids in the kitchen little by little over time.

ACTION POINT

Stop right now to think of ways you can involve your family more in the food process.

PREP HACK #2 - GET THE FAMILY IN ON THE CLEAN-UP – AFTER DINNER

When I cook, I don't clean up as I go. We clean up after dinner. Scandalous, I know—but it speeds up my dinner prep.

There are probably a lot of people who disagree with this (my mother included) and that is A-OK with me. If this method doesn't work for you, I totally understand. Do what works for you—really. But, for me, when I let go of the "clean as I go" way that my mom taught me, it reduced the amount of time I spent cooking dinner and increased the amount of meals I actually cooked at home. So, in the end, it works for me and helps me hit my goals.

I will warn you, that if you come into my kitchen while I'm cooking, it will look semi-explosive. So, there is that. Feel free to do a #hardpass on this step. BUT… if you aren't cooking as many meals at home as you need to be, try this trick and see if it helps you.

PREP HACK #3 - USE A PRESSURE COOKER

I have two pressure cookers and love them to death. I use them all... the... time. They are at the center of simplifying my food routines and reducing my time spent in the kitchen.

It started with one. You know, the brand everyone is buying these days. Bought it on Black Friday for a fire sale price. We fell in love—I used it all the time, and constantly felt myself wishing I had a second one. But no sale prices anywhere on the horizon. So, I did a giant kitchen purge, sold all the extra things I wasn't using, and saved until I could afford a second one. I paid FULL PRICE and have never regretted it. After reading this far in my book, you'll probably understand that if I pay full price for something—especially a duplicate of something I already own—it must yield tremendous benefit.

Why do I love my pressure cooker so much? I thought you would never ask.

1. I CAN CREATE A WIDE ARRAY OF MEALS IN UNDER 60 MINUTES.

As an added bonus, there are a lot of things I can do in only 30 minutes. It takes 30 minutes to pick up take-out!!! So, in the same time I can pick up take-out, I can whip something simple up for everyone to eat. I call this a win–win.

2. EVERYTHING IS HANDS-FREE.

This is a HUGE deal for me (and I imagine it would be for most who are reading this book). There are *a lot* of things that take just as long to cook in the pressure cooker as they do using traditional methods, but with rare exceptions, I don't have to monitor the things I cook in my pressure cooker. I can throw a whole chicken in the pot and go run some errands and come back to a fully-cooked chicken. Even though it takes just as long for me to cook a whole chicken in the pressure cooker (when I account for coming in and out of pressure) as it does in the oven, I can't go run errands while I have my oven running.

3. THE PRESSURE COOKER DRASTICALLY REDUCED THE COOKING TIMES FOR SOME OF MY KITCHEN STAPLES THAT HAVE ESPECIALLY LONG COOKING TIMES WHEN COOKED WITH TRADITIONAL METHODS:

- Dried beans ready in about 60 minutes instead of two days.
- Bone broth ready in about 6 hours instead of 24 hours.
- Steel-cut oats cook in about 15 minutes, completely hands-free.
- Spaghetti squash—that you don't have to cut—cooks in under 30 minutes.
- Homemade marinara sauce can be made in under an hour— and tastes like it has been simmering on the stove all day long.
- You can take something from frozen to table-ready in about 60 minutes. This is perfect for us #forgottotakemeatoutofthefreezer moms.

4. SOME STUFF, IT JUST DOES BETTER.

- You can make hard-boiled eggs that peel flawlessly (Hint: 3-year-olds can peel them independently!).
- You can cook the tastiest refried beans you've ever had.
- It takes cheap meat and turns it into the tastiest of cuts (stew meat, I am looking at you).
- For smaller families, you can cook multiple items in one pot — for instance, rice, beans, and chicken in one pot for a delicious burrito bowl. For our family of 6, this doesn't work well, but I know others really enjoy one-pot meals.

**all times are approximate and include the time it takes to come in and out of pressure.

There are a lot of people out there that use the pressure cooker for amazing and complicated things. I haven't ever done anything fancy in mine. I use mine exclusively for simple staples that I use in my food equations.

I'm pretty sure you can see why I ended up with two. HA! If you pop over to my house, it would not be surprising to see both of my pressure cookers hard at work in my kitchen. I am not one to be easily swayed by kitchen gadget fads. But I can say without a doubt that they have been a blessing to me — reducing my overall food budget and simplifying the time and energy I spend in the kitchen. Is it perfect? Nope! Did it have a fairly large learning curve? Yep! Did it replace all my kitchen appliances? Are you going to see my stove on my curb? Um… no! It's a tool that works for me. If you're currently jammed every day at 4 or 5 and not able to switch that habit around other ways, then it may be worth it for you to consider a pressure cooker.

ACTION POINT

STOP NOW TO CONSIDER WHETHER YOUR FAMILY COULD BENEFIT FROM A PRESSURE COOKER.

If so, start looking for used ones (they really do come up!). If you don't like shopping for used, keep your eye out for sales.

PREP HACK #4 - WHENEVER POSSIBLE...DOUBLE, TRIPLE, OR QUADRUPLE MY ACTIONS

Unless I am in a time crunch, every time that I cook I try to double "something" in the recipe.

Here are some examples of how I do this:

- **When making rice**, I double the portion and freeze the second half.
- **When making something with onions**, I will bust out my food processor, process 4-6 onions, then freeze them in Ziploc bags so I have pre-chopped onion available.
- **When making beans**, I fill up my pressure cooker and freeze the cooked beans in 16 oz. canning jars (the equivalent of a can of beans).
- **When making a casserole**, I make two of them—I either freeze the extra or leave it in the fridge for lunch tomorrow.

- **When making soup**, I double up and plan the extras for lunch the next day.
- **When making a salad**, I chop double the veggies and double the lettuce, so we can have salad the next day for lunch. (Hint: Throw the extra lettuce in a mason jar—it stores so much better in there.)
- **When cooking meat**, I try to ALWAYS double what I cook; I frequently quadruple it.

PREP HACK #5 – WHENEVER POSSIBLE, I SERVE LEFTOVERS FOR LUNCH.

I have covered this in other chapters, but this is such a big deal, I needed to mention it again. This saved me SO MUCH TIME AND ENERGY when I made this switch!

I won't belabor this point here, but if you haven't given this a try yet, TRY IT!!!!

None of these hacks, in and of themselves, will drastically change your life. But layering in a few of them and practicing them intentionally over time will reduce the amount of time and energy you spend in the kitchen.

Chapter 12–Lowering Your Food Bill – The Advanced Version

If you have followed all the steps I have taught you so far on how to lower your grocery bill, and still haven't gotten your food costs low enough to hit your goal, you may need to evaluate your food choices and investigate if there are any cheaper alternatives. I went through this process a few years ago when I wanted to shave an additional $100/month off my bill. Together, my husband and I decided we needed to level up and take our grocery budget through one more cut (This was cut #3 from our original $1200 bill). I had already taken the big steps of setting a budget, paying with cash, finding the cheapest sources of my food, and having a plan. We had already virtually eliminated substitutions, had really simplified our diet, and had dramatically reduced waste by remaining food-flexible. We had made a lot of changes! But to hit our goal of setting aside 15% for retirement, we had to cut another$100/month.

I knew this was going to be more difficult than the first couple rounds of cuts. So, I sat down with my notebook and pen, my favorite beverage, my thinking cap, an open mind, AND my big girl panties. This is a lot of things to sit down with, really. Let's just say the table was full. I sat down to carefully contemplate our food habits and see if there was anything I could tweak to yield additional savings.

HERE ARE SOME OF THE SMALL IDEAS I JOTTED DOWN THAT DAY FOR HOW I COULD LOWER MY BILL EVEN FURTHER:

1. Buy meat with skin and bones
2. Buy whole chickens
3. Buy dried beans rather than canned
4. Buy in bigger bulk
5. Make my own broth
6. Make my own allergen-free baking mixes
7. Choose thighs over breasts
8. Make my own food bars
9. Make my own granola
10. For whoever can eat eggs, serve eggs at breakfast instead of sausage
11. Pop my own popcorn for snacks
12. Cook with whole carrots rather than baby carrots
13. 2-3 mornings a week, make a hash in place of our traditional hash brown and sausages
14. Double up dinners to reheat the leftovers the next day at lunch
15. Buy romaine heads rather than pre-cut lettuce in the bags
16. Grind my own almond butter
17. Make my own almond or coconut milk
18. Replace deli meat with something else for my husband's lunches
19. Try coupons

Honestly, I had to experiment to see if these changes were worth the extra time and energy in balance with the savings they yielded. I tried everything you see listed above (and probably more that I am forgetting). Some of them I decided were absolutely worth the extra effort. With others, after a few attempts, I concluded the savings were not substantial enough to balance the additional effort. Several of them, I now do a combination of—like lettuce, for instance. Sometimes, on busy weeks, I buy a huge bag of pre-cut lettuce because I know I just don't have the extra time for chopping that week. Even though it's more expensive to buy it pre-chopped, it's cheaper than take-out. So, the added expense is worth it to me. Same for canned beans vs. dry beans – some weeks I just need beans in a can. It's about making my food choices reflect the balance of my available resources. When I have more time than money, I can choose more time-intensive ingredients. When I have more money than time, I choose less intensive ingredients. At this stage, for me, this balance is fluid. Which is why I appreciate making my food plan with my calendar in front of me. Notice that all these experiments still fit within my food values. So, when I was looking for cheaper alternatives, I wasn't lowering my food standards, just stretching my mind to include different options.

ACTION POINT

If you have made the basic changes and need to lower your food bill even more, I recommend you do this same exercise that I did.

IF YOU ONLY HAVE 5 MINUTES, schedule an hour to do this activity this week. Mark it on your calendar and slot it for a time.

IF YOU HAVE AN HOUR, sit down with a pen and paper, your favorite beverage, your thinking cap, an open mind, AND your big girl panties. Carefully contemplate your food habits and see if there is anything you can tweak to yield additional savings on your overall food bill.

THINK THROUGH YOUR BREAKFAST HABITS.
Are there any changes you could make, even a couple of days a week, that would reduce your overall breakfast expenses?

THINK THROUGH YOUR LUNCH HABITS.

Are there any changes you could make, even a couple of days a week, that would reduce your overall lunch expenses at home? On the road for you or your family members? Kids' school lunches? Any habits you could change that would reduce the amount you eat out?

THINK THROUGH YOUR DINNER HABITS.

Are there any changes you could make, even a couple of days a week, that would reduce your overall dinner expenses? Any habits you could change that would reduce the amount you eat out?

THINK THROUGH YOUR SNACK HABITS.

Are there any changes you could make, even a couple of days a week, that would reduce your overall snack expenses?

MAKE A PLAN TO IMPLEMENT A HANDFUL OF THESE EXPERIMENTS INTO YOUR NEXT FOOD PLAN. JOT THEM DOWN HERE:

1.
2.
3.
4.
5.

Part 6 – Bonus Chapters

Chapter 13 – Tips for families with Food Allergies

This is written exclusively for families with food allergies. If you don't have food allergies in your home, stop right now for a moment of gratitude, and then quickly move on to Chapter 14. Food allergies are contagious, so you don't want to stay on this page any longer than you must.

My #1 tip for allergen-free peeps to save time and money is to focus on serving food that is naturally allergen-free!

Maybe you're super smart and have already figured this out. But this one took me a looooong time and was at the center of our expensive and complicated food life. When my son was first diagnosed, my goal was to try to re-create all our favorite foods, allergen-free. When you are allergic to dairy, wheat, egg, corn, soy, peanut, pineapple, yeast, beef, and barley, it is not cheap, easy, or tasty to re-create all our favorite foods. Spoiler alert... if you have those allergies and you try to make an allergen-free lasagna, it isn't going to taste very good!!!! And it's probably going to cost you $25. Alternatively, if you decide to cook a grilled chicken breast with a rice pilaf and grilled veggies, you can easily and inexpensively make that allergen-free without losing any of the taste. I have come to realize that most of the allergen substitutions are:

A) BUDGET BUSTERS — There is no getting around the fact that substitute products are blazingly expensive! Flour subs, snack subs, milk subs, bread subs—they're all budget busters. Even when you buy them on sale, they're still expensive.

B) NOT AS HEALTHY — This is personal but remember that I define healthy foods as whole foods. Subs are not whole foods. They're highly processed foods. So, we choose not to have them as a part of our daily food life.

C) NOT AS TASTY —This is also personal, but I feel like a lot of subs leave me wanting. I have yet to find a GF, DF, EF lasagna that I truly love. I have found many that I tolerate. I do, however, love spaghetti squash with a meat marinara, which is naturally free of the Top 8.

d)Time killers – Not always true, but man, it really can be. Anytime I hear the phrase almond flour, I pretty much know it's going to take at least an hour. Can I get a witness? While we're at it, can we all agree that the words almond flour and donuts just... don't... go?

e)More difficult to source — the good allergen substitutes might require that I go to a specialty store. You will remember that, to save time and money, I try to reduce the number of grocery trips that I make. Every time I step into a store, my odds of increasing my grocery budget go up. So, I do my best to stack the odds in my favor by avoiding any extra stops. Specialty health food stores are especially tempting to me, personally, so I reduce these trips as much as possible.

For our day-to-day cooking, the only substitutions we use are butter and milk. This is it. Really. Most of the time, if you saw my cart at the store, you wouldn't even know that we have food allergies.

Avoiding subs on our everyday food saves us time, money, energy, and gives us naturally better-tasting food. When I came to this realization, it literally changed our lives. And our budget. I'm not sure why it took me years.

Does this mean that I never make substitutions? Absolutely not!!! I make subs for all major holidays, for every birthday, and probably about twice a month for special treats. They just aren't a part of our regular, daily food plan. Be on the lookout for my blog posts on my favorite allergen-free special treats. We have found some great ones over the years!

Chapter 14 - Thanks for Coming!

Well—congratulations! You did it! You made it through to the end of this journey. I hope that you took your time, did the exercises along the way, and changed your habits as you went. The only way to create lasting change to your food bill is through consistent and persistent habits—practiced intentionally over time. I wish it were more exciting than that, but it really isn't. And I wish it were something you could focus on one time, and then it would be permanently fixed. But it isn't that either. Like any good thing—a marriage, a business, your job, your kids—your health and your money require maintenance. You must establish good habits, and then maintain them over time to yield the financial results you want.

Even for me, years into taking my food bill seriously, if I am not 'intentional' with my habits, I will slip back into my old take-out habits. If I enter a busy season and I haven't planned for food during that busy time, I will slip back. When this happens, I try not to beat myself up. Mistakes happen. I'm not food-perfect—and I'm not trying to be. Instead, I try to take a step back, regroup, make a food plan that matches this new season, and move forward—learning from the experience. You will have to do the same, because the seasons in your life will shift. Sometimes with no warning. And, with it, your food plan must shift as well.

Don't hesitate to shift your food values and your food formula over time. Don't hesitate to adjust your budget up or down as needed. Maybe you are stepping into a very busy season and have less time in the kitchen than before. Adjusting your budget **UP** to allow for more convenient foods to prepare 'will' save you money in the end.

Maybe you are stepping into a dry season financially and have less money than before. Know that adjusting your budget **DOWN** will require that you increase the time spent shopping for and preparing your foods. **A good food plan balances the time, money, and energy you have available to spend on food *in that season.*** Remember to be honest with yourself about how much time, money, and energy you have to spend on food, and plan accordingly.

It has been a pleasure walking with you on this journey. I hope you stick around. Join our Facebook Group—where other members of the Dinner for a Dollar community hang out and share their tips and tricks for eating whole food on a tight budget. I hang around there frequently sharing my current menus, my most recent fire sale finds, and new ways that I find to creatively use my inexpensive ingredients. Getting plugged in there is a great way for you to maintain the habits you have created while working through the book, so you can work toward your long-term financial goals.

Thank you for trusting me to walk with you. I hope to see you down the road.

Warmly,

Shelly

Acknowledgments

I want to take this time to say a special thank you to all the people who helped make this book a reality. When I say that I couldn't have done this book without you, I literally mean that I could NOT have done this book without you. Seriously. If you are on this page, this book couldn't have happened without you. Thank you. Words can't really tell you how I feel, but I will try.

To Courtney Alderton, my Virtual Business Manager, I want to say that I honestly believe you are an answer to my prayers. I asked God to bring me an assistant that could complete me professionally and He gave me you. You truly are the other half of my brain. I give you words and ideas and you make them adorable, polished, professional, on brand and on time... every single time. Your graphics, designs, and layouts are just gorgeous. Thank you for designing and formatting this book. But, thanks even more for seeing this brand and turning it into a visual reality.

To Angela von Weber-Hahnsberg, my Marketing Director and Copy Editor, I want to say thank you for giving me a vision for how to take this system, turn it into a brand, and share it with the world. You believed in this brand from the beginning and your teaching, guidance, and support along the way has been invaluable. You saw the Big Picture long before I did.

To Megan Fennell, from Housecalls Content Development, I want to say thank you for believing in this project and in me as a writer. As the first person to ever read my book, your belief shaped the direction of this brand. If you hadn't liked it, I am pretty sure we wouldn't be here now. Thank you for your direction and guidance. You shaped the copy and structure of this book in ways I couldn't have visualized.

To my Dad, Paul Hendricks, you taught me everything I know about business. How to dream, how to work, how to serve, and how to push thru—day after day. Thank you for being such a good teacher.

To my Mom and best friend, Elaine Hendricks, you modeled for me, my entire life, what a Proverbs 31 wife should look like. A tireless example of how to be an extraordinary woman. Even at 44, I hope to grow up to be as exceptional as you—while secretly knowing I may not ever fill those shoes. Growing up, you were the ultimate example of how to serve Dinner for a Dollar.

To my kids, thank you for persevering through this project. I know I have been distracted and you all have patiently served and loved me through the process. I know you are all secretly (or not so secretly) glad that the book is finished. I love each of you with my whole heart and can't wait to see what God has for your lives.

Lastly, I want to thank my husband, Kevin Longenecker. Your friendship, partnership, support, and faithfulness throughout our 22 years together is unmatched. That was magnified by this project. You have believed in me and this brand from its' inception and, without that belief and support, I would have never launched. Your patience and flexibility in adjusting to a life with a woman writing a book is an example to all men in how to support their wives. Thank you for loving me well. I wouldn't want to do life with anyone else.

Appendix

If you want the abbreviated version, here is what they have to say:

LEFTOVERS

- Discard any food left out at room temperature for more than 2 hours (1 hour if the temperature was above 90 °F).
- Place food into shallow containers and immediately put in the refrigerator or freezer for rapid cooling.
- Use most cooked leftovers within 3 to 4 days. (See chart.)
- Reheat leftovers to 165 °F.

Cold Storage Chart

Preparation	Type or Description	Refrigerate (40 °F)	Freeze (0 °F)
Beef, Lamb, Pork, Veal			
Fresh beef, lamb, veal and pork	Ground, hamburger, stew meat, variety meat (tongue, liver, heart, kidney, chitterlings)	1-2 days	3-4 months
	Chops, roasts, steaks	3-5 days	4-12 months
	Chops, pre-stuffed	1 day	Does not freeze well
Leftovers	Including casseroles	3-4 days	2-3 months
Corned Beef	In pouch, with pickling juices	5-7 days	Drained, 1 month
Bacon	Bacon	7 days	1 month

Cold Storage Chart

Preparation	Type or Description	Refrigerate (40 °F)	Freeze (0 °F)
Ham (Pre-Cooked)			
Fully Cooked	Slices	3-4 days	1-2 months
	Half	3-5 days	1-2 months
	Whole	7 days	1-2 months
Canned Labeled "Keep Refrigerated"	Opened	3-5 days	1-2 months
	Unopened	6-9 months	Do not freeze
Vacuum sealed	Unopened, fully cooked vacuum sealed, dated	"Use-by" date	1-2 months
	Unopened, fully cooked vacuum sealed, undated	2 weeks	1-2 months

Cold Storage Chart

Preparation	Type or Description	Refrigerate (40 °F)	Freeze (0 °F)
Chicken, Turkey, Other Poultry			
Fresh	Chicken breast, pre-stuffed	1 day	Does not freeze well
	Ground, patties, giblets	1-2 days	3-4 months
	Pieces	1-2 days	1-2 days
	Whole	1-2 days	1 year
Leftovers	Casseroles	3-4 days	4-6 months
	Chicken nuggets, patties	1-2 days	1-3 months
	Pieces, plain or fried	3-4 days	4 months
	Pieces in broth or gravy	3-4 days	6 months

Cold Storage Chart

Preparation	Type or Description	Refrigerate (40 °F)	Freeze (0 °F)
Eggs			
Fresh	In shell	3-5 weeks	Do not freeze
Fresh	Yolk, whites	2-4 days	1 year
Leftovers	Casserole, quiche, omelet	3-4 days	2 months
Leftovers	Hard-cooked	1 week	Does not freeze well
Opened	Liquid pasteurized eggs, egg substitutes	3 days	Does not freeze well
Unopened	Liquid pasteurized eggs, egg substitutes	10 days	1 year

Cold Storage Chart

Preparation	Type or Description	Refrigerate (40 °F)	Freeze (0 °F)
Sausages, Lunch Meats			
Hard Sausage	Jerky sticks, pepperoni	2-3 weeks	1-2 months
Raw Sausage	Beef, chicken, pork, turkey	1-2 days	1-2 months
Smoked Sausage	Breakfast links, patties	7 days	1-2 months
Lunch Meat	Deli-sliced or store-prepared	3-5 days	1-2 months
Opened	Hot dogs	1 week	1-2 months
	Lunch meat—vacuum-packed, sliced	3-5 days	1-2 months
	Summer sausage labeled "keep refrigerated"	3 weeks	1-2 months
Unopened	Hot dogs	2 weeks	1-2 months
	Lunch meat—vacuum-packed, sliced	2 weeks	1-2 months
	Lunch meat—vacuum-packed, sliced	3 months	1-2 months

Cold Storage Chart

Preparation	Type or Description	Refrigerate (40 °F)	Freeze (0 °F)
Seafood			
Fresh	Fish	1-2 days	3-8 months
Fresh	Shellfish	1-2 days	3-12 months
Leftovers	Fish and shellfish	3-4 days	3 months
Miscellaneous			
Frozen Dinners and Entrees	"Keep frozen"	Unsafe to Thaw	3-4 months
Mayonnaise	Commercial, "refrigerate after opening"	2 months	Do Not Freeze
Other Leftovers	Gravy and meat broth	3-4 days	2-3 months
Other Leftovers	Pizza	3-4 days	1-2 months
Other Leftovers	Soups and stews	3-4 days	2-3 months
Other Leftovers	Stuffing	3-4 days	1 month
Salads	Egg, chicken, ham, macaroni, tuna (store-prepared, homemade)	3-5 days	Does Not Freeze Well

Dinner for a Dollar

If you enjoyed this book and found ways to save time, money, or energy on your food because of it, I would love your review on Amazon.

Also, be sure to sign up at https://dinnerforadollar.co/ to receive even more frugal whole food hacks in your email inbox each week. You can also join the One Dollar Dinner Club - the best place to get in on the conversation about saving money on whole foods, with me as your guide!

FREE BONUS MATERIAL!

To follow along with us in the Dinner for a Dollar (DFAD) journey, download free resources, and join the club, be sure to follow the link below and use the code. Your DFAD code is the key to access all the most current material and programs available from DFAD.

Dinnerforadollar.co/member
Code: 55133178326

Here, you can:
- Download the workbook and all the worksheets from the DFAD book.
- Sign up to join the club!
- Connect in a space for people to ask questions, share their struggles and wins as they go through the DFAD system.

These additional materials, teaching and accountability will help increase your results as you move through the book to help you stay on track and hit your food budget goals.

All programs and offerings are subject to change. Check in at the link above for the most current bonus material and programs.

About the Author

Shelly is passionate about helping others create their own personal financial peace - starting with the grocery bill. She is a mom of 4, aged 5-17, whom she raises with her husband, Kevin. She has a master's degree in counseling, however, she has spent the past 17 years focused at home with her kids. In their family, they have 3 diagnosed autoimmune diseases and 4 people with food allergies. She knows firsthand how difficult it can be to feed a large family an allergy-free, whole-food diet on a budget without spending all day in the kitchen. Over the past 10 years, Shelly has created her own system that has helped her reduce her grocery bill by $12,000 a year, and now wants to share it with the world.

She enjoys sharing how she feeds her family Dinner for a Dollar not only through her book, but also through speaking engagements and one-on-one coaching. You can book her at www.dinnerforadollar.co. There, you can also sign up to get her weekly frugal whole-food hacks emails or connect with her through Facebook at www.facebook.com/dinnerforadollar.